Essential Histories

The First World War (4)
The Mediterranean Front 1914–1923

Essential Histories

The First World War (4)

The Mediterranean Front 1914–1923

Michael Hickey

OSPREY
PUBLISHING

First published in Great Britain in 2002 by Osprey Publishing,
Elms Court, Chapel Way, Botley, Oxford OX2 9LP, UK
Email: info@ospreypublishing.com

ISBN 1 84176 373 X

Editor: Rebecca Cullen
Design: Ken Vail Graphic Design, Cambridge, UK
Cartography by The Map Studio
Index by Alison Worthington
Picture research by Image Select International
Origination by Grasmere Digital Imaging, Leeds, UK
Printed and bound in China by L. Rex Printing Company Ltd.

02 03 04 05 06   10 9 8 7 6 5 4 3 2 1

For a complete list of titles available from Osprey Publishing
please contact:

Osprey Direct UK, PO Box 140,
Wellingborough, Northants, NN8 2FA, UK.
Email: info@ospreydirect.co.uk

Osprey Direct USA, c/o MBI Publishing,
PO Box 1, 729 Prospect Ave
Osceola, WI 54020, USA.
Email: info@ospreydirectusa.com

www.ospreypublishing.com

This book is one of four titles on the First World War in the
Osprey Essential Histories series

Contents

Introduction

The 1914–18 war was ultimately decided on the Western Front in France and Belgium, and on the Eastern Front, although the relentless submarine campaign waged by the Imperial German navy on the high seas against both Allies and neutrals came close to winning the war for the Central Powers in 1917. Other struggles on the periphery brought the final disintegration and elimination of the Ottoman and Austro-Hungarian empires. The most important of these took place around the Mediterranean, where the strategic and political fortunes of the different countries on both sides had long been involved.

With the Adriatic, Aegean and Ionian seas the Mediterranean covers over a million square miles of water and a series of campaigns were fought around its shores: in

HMS *Albion* aground off Gapa Tepe, Gallipoli, during preliminary bombardment; HMS *Canopus* closing in to tow her off; both ships under close-range fire from Turkish batteries ashore. Both ships were pre-dreadnoughts, carrying four 12-inch guns as main armament. At less than 13,000 tons displacement they were regarded as 'light' battleships, primarily for maintaining a presence on the world's sea routes rather than in the main fleet battle line. *Canopus*, although launched after the first of the dreadnoughts and thus obsolete from her laying-down, had played a part, anchored as guardship in Port Stanley harbour, when Admiral Sturdee, caught there whilst coaling by von Spee's squadron in December 1914, got up steam and emerged to sink the *Scharnhorst* and *Gneisenau* in a running battle for which the battleship was too slow. (IWM)

the Balkans, on the Gallipoli peninsula and the Dardanelles, in Palestine, in northern Italy; and even in the remote deserts of Arabia and along the Tigris and Euphrates rivers. The Turks, humiliated in a series of short but bloody wars in the years immediately preceding 1914, were seriously underestimated by the Allies ranged against them, but fought heroically and successfully in defence of their native soil at Gallipoli and in the Dardanelles, and inflicted serious reverses on their enemies elsewhere. But in the end the loss of Baghdad, of Jerusalem and Damascus sealed the fate of the Ottoman Empire and gave a formerly obscure Turkish officer, Mustafa Kemal, the opportunity to raise a new Turkish state from the ashes of defeat. The young dominions of Australia and New Zealand gave freely of their manpower to the Middle East campaigns and at Gallipoli forged their own national identities. New Arab nations emerged and the shifting frontiers of the Balkan states created as the result of post-war treaties would lead to future problems, unimagined at the time.

The causes of the First World War included France's desire for revenge for the humiliations of 1870–71, rising German militarism, and the realisation of Germany's leaders that their newly-unified nation had been left far behind in the rush for empire pursued successfully by Britain and France. In the Mediterranean theatre other factors entered the equation. Nationalism and particularly Pan-Slavism were strong in the disparate provinces of the Austrian Empire, notably in the Balkans, and Arab nationalism was stirring within the Ottoman territories; age-old suspicions simmered between Slav and Muslim, and there were historic rivalries between Turkey and her neighbour Russia. Frequent shifts of power and the strings of treaties eagerly drawn up by the meddling chancelleries of Europe throughout the 19th century had contributed to the general instability. The opening of the Suez Canal in 1869 and its purchase by Britain in 1875 drove British foreign policy in the Near East for the next century, providing the excuse

Cartoon drawing of General Sir Frederick Maude at the time of his appointment as commander in Mesopotamia, holding the 'Key to the East'. Maude took over command at a low ebb in British fortunes, but as the result of meticulous staff work, sound logistics, and the improvement in morale wrought by his own personality, he reversed the course of the campaign, beat the Turks and their German advisers, and captured Baghdad – where he was fated to die, of cholera, in the house where the German commander von der Goltz had also met his end. (IWM)

for British domination over Egypt even though it was nominally part of the Ottoman Empire.

A strong British garrison had been based on the Suez Canal since 1882. While the Ottoman state remained supine and in terminal decay there seemed little risk to the canal's security. But as German eyes turned eastwards and the influence of Berlin enveloped the Turkish establishment, it became clear that there was a more immediate danger to India than that posed by Imperial Russia, whose ambitions had been curtailed since her defeat by Japan in the war of 1904–1905.

Another empire was also in trouble by the beginning of the 20th century. After the dissolution of the Holy Roman Empire in 1806 the House of Habsburg had ruled territories including Bohemia, Hungary, Transylvania, Croatia, Galicia, and the Italian provinces of Venezia and Lombardy. This polyglot empire was run by the Catholic Church, the army, a pervasive secret police apparatus, and a vast civil service. When the Emperor Ferdinand abdicated in 1848, the 'year of revolutions', his successor, the 18-year-old Francis Joseph, was immediately confronted by independence movements in all directions. Having survived that crisis, but defeated in 1866 at Sadowa and Magenta by the Piedmontese and their Prussian allies, Francis Joseph decreed a new constitution. The *Ausgleich* or Compromise of 1867 created an Austro-Hungarian dual monarchy. Despite granting a degree of autonomy to Hungary the new constitution did little to quell rising tides of nationalism as Croats, Serbs, Romanians and the Czechs of Moravia continued to assert their rights.

As the Emperor addressed these problems, the Ottoman grip over the Balkans and Near East steadily slackened. From Berlin a succession of hard-headed statesmen and the Kaisers they served looked with increasing interest at the prospect before them. They sought political control over the route from central Europe across the Balkans to Constantinople, thence through Asia Minor, Arabia and Mesopotamia and on to the

The opposing sides, 1914–18

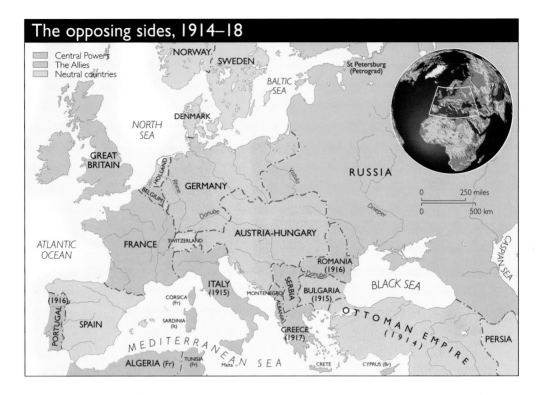

Central Powers
The Allies
Neutral countries

NORWAY
SWEDEN
BALTIC SEA
St Petersburg (Petrograd)
NORTH SEA
DENMARK
GREAT BRITAIN
HOLLAND
BELGIUM
GERMANY
Rhine
Vistula
RUSSIA
Dnieper
0   250 miles
0   500 km
ATLANTIC OCEAN
Danube
FRANCE
SWITZERLAND
AUSTRIA-HUNGARY
ROMANIA (1916)
CASPIAN SEA
ITALY (1915)
Danube
MONTENEGRO
SERBIA
BULGARIA (1915)
BLACK SEA
(1916)
CORSICA (Fr)
ALBANIA
PORTUGAL
SPAIN
SARDINIA (It)
GREECE (1917)
OTTOMAN EMPIRE (1914)
PERSIA
MEDITERRANEAN SEA
ALGERIA (Fr)
TUNISIA (Fr)
Malta
CRETE
CYPRUS (Br)

Persian Gulf. Beyond lay the covetable British Indian Empire. The Suez Canal, linking Britain to the Indian Raj and beyond to Singapore, Australia, and New Zealand, was the strategic prize.

By the end of the first decade of the 20th century the world was ripe for war. In Europe the great powers each endeavoured through a network of treaties to maintain a favourable equilibrium of power. On one side, Britain, France and Imperial Russia; on the other, the Central Powers, Germany and Austria-Hungary; joined somewhat tentatively by Italy to form the Triple Alliance. Further afield, in the Balkans and Near East, a series of open powder barrels awaited only the dropping of a casual spark to set off a train of fatal explosions.

Chronology

1908   Austria-Hungary annexes Bosnia-Herzegovina.

1911–12   Loss of Turkish North African provinces to Italy.

1912–13   Balkan Wars. Further Turkish defeats.

1914   **28 June** Assassination of Archduke Franz Ferdinand and his wife at Sarajevo.
28 July Francis Joseph signs declaration of war against Serbia.
3 August Turkey declares 'armed neutrality'. Germany declares war on France.
4 August Britain declares war on Germany, and Germany invades Belgium.
5 August Austria declares war on Russia, and Montenegro declares war on Austria.
6 August Serbia declares war on Germany.
10 August France declares war on Austria-Hungary.
12 August Austrians invade Serbia. Britain declares war on Austria-Hungary.
31 August Greece formally declares neutrality.
1 October Turkey closes Dardanelles.
1 November Turkey declares war on Anglo-French Entente.
2 November Russia and Serbia declare war on Turkey.
5 November Britain and France declare war on Turkey.
11 November Ottoman Sultan, as Caliph of Islam, proclaims *jihad* against Britain and France.
30 December Russia appeals to London for a diversionary attack to be made against Turkey.

1915   **3 February** Turks fail to cross Suez Canal.
19 February Allied fleet begins bombardment of outer forts at the Dardanelles.
18 March Anglo-French naval attack on the Chanak Narrows repulsed with loss of three battleships, damage to others.
25 April Anglo-French forces go ashore at Helles, and at Kum Kale on Asiatic shore.
23 May Italian Government declares war on Austria.
4 August Allied reconnaissance party arrives at Salonika to assess port and railway facilities.
6 August Start of great Allied attack at Gallipoli; further landings made at Suvla Bay after dark.
10 August Turkish counter-attack at Gallipoli drives British and New Zealanders off high ground.
20 August Italy declares war on Turkey.
21 September Greek premier Venizelos calls for massive Allied reinforcement of Salonika as condition for Greek entry into war.
27 September Greek King Constantine consents to Allied force landing at Salonika.
1 October British advance party arrives at Salonika.
5 October Combined German-Austrian attack on Belgrade begins.
9 October Belgrade falls to German-Austrian attack. Austrians invade Montenegro.
11 October Bulgarian troops invade Serbia.
14 October Mutual declarations of war between Serbia and Bulgaria.

Serbs retreat towards
Albanian frontier.
12 December Allied navies begin
evacuation of Serb army from Albania
as Bulgars close in on Salonika defences.
19 December Evacuation of the Anzac
and Suvla beach-heads at Gallipoli in
one night without casualties.

1916 **8 January** Successful completion of
Gallipoli evacuation at Helles.
10 January Completion of Allied
'Entrenched Camp' at Salonika.
29 April Mesopotamia: Fall of
Kut with 13,309 British and
Indian prisoners plus over
3,000 non-combatants.
5 June Arabia: Sherif Hussein starts
Arab Revolt at Medina, proclaims
independence of Hedjaz.
7 July Lloyd George succeeds
Kitchener (drowned en route to
Russia) as War Minister.
1 September Britain and France
secretly sign the Sykes-Picot
agreement on post-war partition of
the Ottoman Empire.
11 October Allies disarm Greek fleet.
Riots in Athens in protest at
Allied action.
21 November Emperor Francis
Joseph dies, aged 86, succeeded by his
great-nephew Charles.
23 November Greek provisional
government at Salonika declares war
on Germany and Bulgaria.
1 December Fighting in Athens
between royalist troops and
Anglo-French detachments.
7 December London: Lloyd George
becomes prime minister.

1917 **5–7 January** Allied conference in
Rome to discuss priorities for
campaigns in Italy and Salonika.
20 February as campaign in Arabia
gathers momentum, first attack on
Hedjaz railway by Arab irregulars.
11 March Baghdad falls to
General Maude.

26 March Palestine: 1st battle of
Gaza.
17 April Palestine: 2nd battle of Gaza
– Despite use of tanks, momentum
lost and attack stalls.
5 May Allies launch major offensive
in Macedonia but fail to get Serb
co-operation.
12 June King Constantine of Greece
abdicates after Allied ultimatum,
succeeded by younger son Alexander;
British and French troops land
at Piraeus.
26 June Venizelos confirmed by
Allies as prime minister.
2 July Greece declares war on the
Central Powers. In Arabia, Colonel
Lawrence and Arab irregulars attack
Hedjaz railway and Turkish garrisons.
12 September Italy: New German
14th Army under General von Below
deploys on Isonzo front.
24 October Battle of Caporetto;
Austro-German attack breaks Italian
2nd Army.
29 October General Cadorna orders
retreat to line of river Piave.
31 October Italians back behind river
Tagliamento. In Palestine, Allenby
opens 3rd battle of Gaza.
5 November Allies confer at
Rapallo as Italians ask for 15 Allied
divisions.
9 November General Diaz replaces
Cadorna as Italian C-in-C.
14 November Allenby resumes
advance on Jerusalem, which falls on
9 December.
22 December Salonika: new Allied
C-in-C, General Guillaumat, replaces
Sarrail. Austrians fail to break through
on the river Piave as astonishing revival
in Italian national morale takes place.

1918 **1 February** Austrian navy mutinies
at Cattaro.
14 September Final Allied offensive
starts in Macedonia with battle of the
River Vardar. Mutinies break out in
Bulgarian army.

19 September Palestine: Allenby fights and wins battle of Megiddo. RAF aircraft destroy the Turkish 7th Army in defiles of Wadi Fara.

23 September British capture Acre and Haifa.

26 September Bulgaria seeks peace terms as mutinous troops march on Sofia to declare a republic. Armistice signed on 29 September after talks at Salonika.

1 October Allenby and Lawrence arrive simultaneously at Damascus.

24 October Allies attack on a wide front and win battle of Vittorio Veneto, followed by rout of Austrian army with mass desertions of Czech, Serb, Croat, and Polish troops.

30 October Ottoman Empire sues for peace, signs armistice on.

3 November Austria signs armistice.

1919 **8 January** General Milne appointed C-in-C at Constantinople with garrison of 35,000 troops.

3 February Venizelos outlines Greek claims to Smyrna at Versailles.

13 May Greek troops land at Smyrna, ostensibly to protect Christians but extend their holding to include large tracts of hinterland.

22 May Turkey: Kemal issues his 'Amasya Decisions', calling for new national government.

28 May first clash between Greeks and Turks, at Odmis.

21 June Angora (Ankara) Kemal declares independence from Ottoman government.

11 July Ottoman government outlaws Kemal, who is elected president by new Turkish National Congress on 23 July.

27 November Kemal sets up Nationalist Council of Representatives at Angora (renamed Ankara).

1920 **16 March** Allies tighten occupation of Constantinople. Massacres of Armenians by Turks continue.

18 March last meeting of Imperial Ottoman Parliament.

23 April Turkey: Grand National Assembly convenes at Ankara and forms new government.

25 April League of Nations Mandates for Palestine and Mesopotamia announced, Palestinian Arabs attack British troops and Jewish settlers.

22 June Greeks launch offensive in Anatolia against Turkish Nationalist forces and advance to Usak, 120 miles east of Smyrna.

25 July Greek forces occupy Adrianople in Turkish Thrace.

10 August Treaty of Sevres: Greece is awarded Turkish Thrace and the Turkish Aegean islands, and five-year control of Smyrna and its hinterland pending a plebiscite. Syria, Mesopotamia, Armenia and Arabia recognised as independent; the Dardanelles and Bosphorus to be demilitarised and administered by the League of Nations and all Turkish claims to former Ottoman lands inhabited by non-Turkish peoples to be renounced. Turkish army to be reduced to a cadre of 50,000. Greeted with fury in Turkey. Nationalists refuse to accept the Treaty and go to war with the Greeks.

1923 Following the Treaty of Lausanne, replacing the Treaty of Sevres, the Allies evacuate Constantinople on 23 August.

The road to war

To understand the complex factors affecting the Mediterranean war it is necessary to look into the histories of the numerous nations involved. Many of the conflicts can be traced back to the middle ages and beyond. The Ottoman empire arose from the fall of the eastern Christian Empire in 1453 and the vigour of militant Islam. Successive sultans' armies fought their way westward, by 1529 to the gates of Vienna; bringing whole provinces of the Balkans, Arabia, North Africa and much of the Iberian peninsula

Quinine parade for British troops in the field. The revolting taste of the medicine made it difficult to enforce health discipline and the only answer was to hold compulsory parades such as this, at which the troops are not slow to show their reluctance. Malaria in a particularly virulent form caused more casualties to British troops than combat in this theatre. (IWM)

under Ottoman rule. Vienna, however, saw the first serious reverse; a Turkish army of some 120,000 men under Suleiman the Magnificent was repulsed by the city's 16,000 defenders and with the raising of that siege the Ottoman military machine began slowly to decline. In 1683 it reached Vienna again, to be defeated with enormous loss by 70,000 Christians. Ottoman sea power in the Mediterranean was broken in 1571 at Lepanto when the Venetian and Spanish battle fleets shattered the Turks in the last great battle fought by oar-propelled ships.

The Ottoman decline was irreversible. The empire had overrun many Christian states and these territories were in continual turmoil, their struggles for independence aided, when it suited them, by the western powers. The Orthodox Christian Slav population of Serbia

Serbia and Salonika, 1914–16

AUSTRIA-HUNGARY
ROMANIA
□ Bucharest
Belgrade (Beograd)
Orsova
BOSNIA
Jadar
Drina
Morava
Danube
Sarajevo
SERBIA
Nis (Nish)
□ Sofia
BULGARIA
HERZE-GOVINA
Mitrovica
Pristina
MONTENEGRO
Cattaro
KOSSOVO
Struma
THRACE
Scutari
Uskub (Skopje)
Veles
Lake Doiran
Fort Rupel
Kavalla
Durazzo (Durrës)
Tirana
Monastir
Crna
Vardar
MACEDONIA
Thasos
Salonika
Samothrace
Imbros
Dardanelles
Chanak
ADRIATIC SEA
ALBANIA
AEGEAN SEA
Lemnos
N
Straits of Otranto
Voyusa
Valona
GREECE
THESSALY
Corfu
Ionnina

General disposition of Serb armies, late Oct 1915
Serb Position, late Nov 1915
Evacuation of Serb armies Jan–Feb 1916
Front line, Dec 1916–Sept 1918
Allied 'Entrenched Camp', Dec 1915–Apr 1916
Initial Austro-Hungarian thrusts, Oct 1915
Final German/Austrian offensive 1916

0   100 miles
0   200 km

gained autonomy in 1817 and 12 years later Russian pressure and the participation of idealistic individuals – notably Lord Byron – enabled Greece to break away from Constantinople. There was growing concern in London over increasing Russian influence in the Balkans, where Pan-Slavism, the awareness of the brotherhood of Slavs, fuelled rebellion against Ottomans and Austrians alike. Russia backed this movement, and was seen throughout the 19th century as a threat to British interests in India. In Vienna there was alarm at the rise of Pan-Slavism on the doorstep, especially as Austria had enough problems of its own among its non-Germanic populations. France favoured the Christian populations of the Levant, supported them in their struggles to escape from the Turks, and

sought to colonise sub-Saharan and North Africa. French advisers helped the remarkable Pasha Mehmet Ali to become ruler of Egypt in 1806. In 1823 his French-trained army pushed south into the Sudan to found Khartoum. Mehmet's son Ibrahim, defying orders from Constantinople (as had his father), moved north and took Damascus in 1832, defeated a Turkish army sent to bring him to book, and headed for Constantinople. Hurried discussions between Austrian and Russian diplomats led to the Treaty of Umkiar Skelessi which appointed Russia as military protector of Turkey, with the right to close the Dardanelles to warships of any other power. But Britain and France regarded the treaty with dismay and resolved to get it abolished or at least revised as soon as possible.

In 1839 the Turkish sultan Mahmoud II died, having failed to recover Syria from Ibrahim. The great powers hurried to take advantage of the Ottoman decline but disagreed as to how they should act, all having their own selfish objectives. France was keen to install the ageing Mehmet as hereditary ruler of Syria and Egypt but the Foreign Office in London saw a dangerous opening for Russian expansion in the direction of India. Palmerston, the British Foreign Secretary, produced a formula acceptable to Russia, Prussia and Austria whereby Mehmet was granted the hereditary right to rule over Egypt and (if he agreed immediately) the administration of Syria for life. The French, his patrons, were excluded from the deal and objected vehemently; Mehmet declined the offer but was nonetheless granted government of Egypt. France was re-admitted to the club and a new treaty was drafted to replace that of Umkiar Skelessi: the Treaty of London, signed in 1840, under which the Dardanelles and Bosphorus remained closed to all foreign warships *as long as the Ottoman Empire stayed peaceful*. Palmerston's crafty diplomacy had successfully scrapped the older treaty and displaced Russian influence in Turkey, which now enjoyed 12 years of relative peace. The sultan, gaining confidence, supported reforms of the civil service and military systems and declared the equality of all citizens of the empire. But corruption remained endemic and religious fanaticism continued to deny the large Christian population their rights. In 1852 the new French Emperor, Napoleon III, decided to assert himself by insisting that France should have guardianship of the holy places in Palestine, hitherto in the custody of the Orthodox churches. In response Tsar Nicholas, who detested the upstart Napoleon, told the Turks to acknowledge Russian protection of the Orthodox church throughout the empire, including the Balkans.

Nicholas, (who coined the expression that the Turkish empire was 'the sick man of Europe'), then suggested an Anglo-Russian partition of the tottering empire. Rebuffed by Palmerston, Nicholas ordered his troops into the provinces of Wallachia and Moldavia. As war loomed, the French and British fleets entered the Dardanelles. Turkey declared war on Russia in October 1853 and immediately lost a disastrous naval encounter with the Russians at Sinope. The Anglo-French fleet entered the Black Sea in January 1854, and the two nations went to war with Russia two months later in support of Turkey in what became known later as the Crimean War. The war ended with a treaty signed at Paris in 1856. The Ottoman decline continued. Wallachia and Moldavia achieved autonomy and became Rumania under a German prince, Charles of Hohenzollern, who reigned wisely as Carol I until 1914.

Ottoman rule eventually broke down in Syria with civil war following a massacre of Maronite Christians by Druse Muslims, which gave the opportunistic Napoleon III another chance to assert himself. A French army savagely put down the Druse in Lebanon, and a Christian governor was appointed. In Greece, independent since 1833, there was a rebellion against King Otto, a Bavarian, and he was replaced by King George I of the Hellenes, a Dane, who reigned from 1863 to 1913 when he was assassinated in Salonika. George was succeeded by his son Constantine, whose wife Sophia was the sister of Kaiser Wilhelm II of Germany. Constantine was educated in Germany and attended the Prussian Military Academy. As a professional soldier he served with distinction in the Balkan Wars but his pro-German sympathies lay uneasily with his professed neutrality on the outbreak of war in 1914.

Rebellion against Ottoman rule continued to spread in the latter half of the 19th century. Limited self-rule was granted to the Cretans following an uprising in 1863, and in 1867 the Turks abandoned seven great fortresses in Serbia. A revolt in Herzegovina in 1875 spread like wildfire through Bosnia, Serbia, Montenegro and Bulgaria. Austria, Russia and Germany now put pressure on the Sublime Porte, the seat of Ottoman government in Constantinople (in what was termed the 'Berlin Memorandum') to implement

long-overdue reforms under threat of armed
intervention by the signatory powers. Britain
firmly declined to join in, and the 'Concert
of Europe' failed. The results were
calamitous. Serbia and Montenegro declared
war on Turkey, a revolution in
Constantinople deposed the Sultan, and
Turkish troops massacred thousands of
Bulgars. In London, Gladstone called for the
expulsion of the Turks 'bag and baggage'
from Europe. A new sultan, Murad V, was
swiftly deposed in turn and replaced by
Abdul Hamid ('The Damned') who was to
reign until 1909. His refusal to grant
autonomy to his Christian provinces and
implement reform led to a declaration of war
by Russia in April 1877. Rumania,
Montenegro and Serbia gladly joined in and
by December that year Russian troops were
within sight of Constantinople. Under the
terms of the Treaty of San Stefano, signed in
March 1878, independence was granted to
Serbia, Montenegro, Rumania and Bulgaria,
including Macedonia.

Crown Prince Charles of Austria-Hungary inspects a
German guard of honour. Following the assassination of
his uncle, the Archduke Franz Ferdinand at Sarajevo in
1914 Charles became heir presumptive to the dual
Imperial throne, succeeding to it as Karl I in 1916 on the
death of the aged emperor Francis Joseph. The new
Austrian parliament deposed him in 1919 and he went
into exile in Switzerland, dying in 1922. (IWM)

The victorious partners immediately fell
out over the division of the spoils. Once
more there was alarm in western Europe and
Britain's prime minister Disraeli ordered the
Mediterranean Fleet through the Dardanelles.
Russia was persuaded to modify the San
Stefano Treaty at the Congress of Berlin in
the summer of 1878 (The Berlin Treaty) but
Turkey still had to grant Serbia, Montenegro
and Rumania their independence. Russia
acquired Bessarabia, Kars in eastern Anatolia,
and Batum. Bosnia and Herzegovina passed
under Austrian protection and Bulgaria was
partitioned in two. Macedonia remained
Turkish. Under a separate convention Britain
garrisoned and administered Cyprus and

guaranteed the sultan's remaining Asian territories. The Berlin Congress was a way-point in the disintegration of the Ottoman Empire. Eleven million Christians were freed from Ottoman rule at a stroke and 30 years of peace in the Middle East ensued. Turkey's outstations were there for the picking by opportunists and France took over in Tunis in 1881. Britain, having defeated the Egyptian army at Tel-el-Kebir in 1882, established a *de facto* government over Egypt to protect the Suez Canal. A string of inter-Balkan agreements brought about a series of border re-alignments that Turkey was now too feeble to prevent. None of the treaties prevented the bellicose Serbs from taking up arms against Bulgaria, to be soundly beaten in a two-week campaign. The Bulgars were in turn threatened by the Austrians and their ruler Prince Alexander was forced to resign in 1886, to be replaced by yet another spare German prince, Ferdinand of Saxe-Coburg. Closely related to Queen Victoria, he ruled with moderation, restyling himself as Tsar in 1908. Serbia fell prey to blood feuds, the Obrenovitch family coming to a grisly end in 1903 when the king and his morganatic queen Draga were slaughtered in their palace by dissident army officers. The rival Karageorgevitch family took over the throne.

Greece went to war again with Turkey in 1897 over Muslim persecution of Cretan Christians, but the fighting was stopped by the great powers when it seemed the Turks were about to win.

Turkey's situation in 1900 was unhappy. Of the Sultan's remaining subjects no less than four million were Christians of one sort or other. Although Austria now occupied Bosnia and Herzegovina the Sultanate still regarded them and Bulgaria as Turkish lands. Balkan history was still affected by resonances of the battle of Kossovo in 1398, when the Turks under Murad I had destroyed the combined forces of Serbia, Bosnia and Albania. Kossovo, with its predominantly Muslim population, remained an almost holy place for Serbs and the mythology surrounding the disaster of 1398 sustains their national identity to this day. The result of that battle ensured Turkish political, cultural and religious domination of Kossovo for the next six centuries.

Another side-effect of the Berlin Treaty was a resurgence of Pan-Slavism as Croats, Slovenes and Montenegrins who had shed Turkish rule sought to join hands with their Serb brethren and the ethnic South Slavs of Bosnia-Herzegovina. The concept of a greater Serbia struck dread into Austrians, Hungarians and Turks alike and threatened to antagonise Bulgaria, which nurtured designs on the assorted population of Macedonia and (more alarmingly) on Greece.

In Turkey a new political force was at work, threatening the old regime. The new constitution of 1878 drafted by the Grand Vizier Midhat Pasha had promised widespread civil liberties and parliamentary government, but the Sultan saw to it that the western-style parliament (the first of its kind in an Islamic country) only convened once. A new, educated middle-class began to feel its strength, breeding the Young Turk movement, which instrumental in firing the revolution of 1908 which forced the revival of the Midhat constitution that followed. The leader of the Young Turks was an army officer, Enver Bey, ably assisted by a small group who all became ministers in the government he led in 1914 when it brought Turkey into the war on the side of the Central Powers. All of them came to violent ends in the years immediately following the war.

The *Putsch* instigated by the Young Turks triggered several reactions. Bulgaria declared independence, Austria annexed Bosnia-Herzegovina and neither sought representation in the Ottoman Parliament promised under the Midhat constitution. Ripples spread out from Constantinople: the Serbs mobilised, and early in 1909 Berlin warned the Russians – Bulgaria's sponsors – to recognise the Austrian annexation, implying that failure to comply would involve war with both Germany and Austria-Hungary. Russia and Serbia took the hint; but it was clear for all to see that Germany was prepared to invade Belgium and France, using Balkan instability as an excuse. Britain's answer was to lay the keels of eight dreadnoughts instead of the four or six originally budgeted for in the 1909 Naval Estimates. War was in the air, and Russia, France and Britain nervously closed ranks. Italy, formerly bound to Germany and Austria by the Triple Alliance Treaty of 1882, began to shuffle aside, her leaders knowing full well that she was utterly unprepared for a major war. In Austria the 'War Party', in which Count Berchthold the foreign minister was a moving spirit, urged the emperor to attack the Serbs at once before the Russians could mobilise for their protection.

Italy's position at this time was nominally governed by her membership of the Triple Alliance, which she had entered into primarily out of concern about France. Progressively revised over the years the terms of the alliance came to embrace North Africa, but in 1902 the Italians and French had come secretly to a compact by which, in return for a free hand in Tripolitania, Italy declared that its share in the Triple Alliance was *not* directed at France. Austria's annexation of Bosnia-Herzegovina in 1908 complicated things. It implied that Italy would join the Central Powers in war against France. Neither the Germans nor the Austrians believed that the Italians could be relied on. When in 1895 Graf von Schlieffen drafted his celebrated plan for the subjugation of France he based it on the assumption that the Italians would do no more than face the French from their home ground on the heights of Piedmont. At

the German Imperial manoeuvres of 1913 the Kaiser tried in vain to extract a promise from General Pollo, the Italian Chief of Staff, that in the event of general war Italy would commit no less than five army corps to the upper Rhine. As late as February 1914 Pollo confirmed the deployment of three army corps and two cavalry divisions against France. But nothing came of this. In 1914 General Pollo died. His successor, General Count Luigi Cadorna, found that the army was in no state to fight any sort of war, having used up most of its equipment in the North African campaign of 1911–12. Cadorna faced a gigantic task of modernisation and reorganisation before the army could meet the role he had in mind – no less than the invasion and defeat of Austria. Italy lacked the raw materials required for a war industry. Short of all types of ammunition and without

General Count Luigi Cadorna, born in 1850 into one of the old Piedmontese families that had traditionally been at the heart of the Italian military elite, he was appointed Chief of Staff in 1914 to face the problems of reinvigorating an army depleted in strength by its recent north African campaign. He was forced to lead it in war from 1915 despite its manifest inadequacies of equipment and training. Believing that offensive action alone held the key to victory he persisted in launching a succession of bloody assaults on the Austrians in the Isonzo sector. Arrogant, ruthless with his subordinates and unapproachable by his troops, to whom he was merely a remote figure, he was removed from command following the catastrophic defeat of the Italians at Caporetto in 1917. (IWM)

the medium and heavy artillery required to tackle the formidable Austrian border defences, she opted for neutrality in August 1914. There were two valid excuses for this apparent breach of faith: a secret clause in the Triple Alliance treaty absolved the Italians from fighting the British, and under Article 7 Austria undertook to consult the Italian government before taking any military action in the Balkans. The invasion of Serbia in 1914 by the Austro-Hungarian army justified Italy's neutrality and this neutrality was the signal for which the French and British governments had been waiting. Italy's entry into the war on their side in 1915 was the result of energetic work by politicians and diplomats to produce a deal politically and financially acceptable in Rome.

The decay of the Ottoman Empire was carefully monitored in Berlin where finely judged diplomacy ensured that the Sultan, however unpopular, retained his throne as long as his friendship with Germany lasted. Turkey's tottering economy was sustained by hard-headed loans like that granted to construct the Turkish section of the Berlin–Baghdad railway, a key element in German strategic planning. Help was given from the 1880s in training and equipping the Turkish army but it was not until 1913 that a full training mission was sent from Germany, under the formidable General Otto Liman von Sanders. Kaiser Wilhelm II paid two state visits to Constantinople in the 1880s and 1890s and the diplomats selected as German ambassadors to the Sublime Porte were men of the highest calibre.

The opposing armies

Britain

Having successfully avoided involvement in European wars since 1815, British defence policy in 1914 relied on a strong navy to secure the sea lanes and deny them to Germany. The fleet, recently assembled for the royal review at Spithead, was ready for war. Its reservists were in post and the fleet fully armed and bunkered. The Grand (or main battle) Fleet was held in home waters to deal with any attempt by the German High Seas Fleet to break out from its home bases, to provide defence against invasion and to support other naval forces in home waters. Of the nine naval commands for overseas waters, tasked with keeping the sea lanes open, foremost was the prestigious Mediterranean Fleet based at Malta.

The Royal Navy enjoyed the status earned by its stupendous performance during the Napoleonic wars, but was professionally conservative. When Britain went to war with Russia in 1853 the battle line still consisted of wooden battleships scarcely distinguishable from Nelson's *Victory*, carrying up to 120 muzzle-loading cannon and a full set of sails. Although the newer ones were fitted with steam propulsion, the very idea of this innovation was anathema to many older admirals. When Fisher, destined to be the most innovative 1st Sea Lord of all time,

An ambulance wagon makes its way up Gully Ravine, Helles, at the height of the Gallipoli Campaign. Earlier in the summer of 1915 this had been the scene of savage fighting. Sudden downpours of rain turned the normally dry watercourse into a raging torrent, and afterwards all traffic had to contend with deep mud. (IWM)

joined the service as a midshipman in 1854 he was signed in by the last of Nelson's captains. As he rose steadily through the ranks his ambition and ability secured accelerated promotion. A gunnery officer in the fleet as it passed through the Dardanelles in 1878, he had carefully noted the fixed batteries guarding the Chanak Narrows. As he successively occupied the key posts in the navy's hierarchy his vision turned the service on its head, forcing the adoption of the torpedo, steam turbines, oil fuel, mines, submarines, wireless, and most importantly the all-big-gun dreadnought battleship. On his way he made many enemies, for he waged ferocious vendettas. When he retired in 1910, Britain had achieved a superiority in capital ships over all other European nations, with a 60 per cent lead over Germany. In August 1914 Britain possessed 24 dreadnoughts with another 13 under construction, to Germany's 13 and 10 on the stocks. Counting pre-dreadnoughts, some of which dated back to the early 1890s and were unfit for the line of battle, the Royal Navy could boast a total of 65 battleships.

The other category of capital ship was the battle cruiser (a concept developed by Fisher), designed for high speed and heavy armament, albeit at the cost of armoured protection, for hunting German commerce raiders and acting as scouts for the main battle fleet. Britain had one of these, armed with 12 inch or 13.5 inch guns.

Discounting a mass of ancient armoured and light cruisers designed for colonial protection duties, there were 16 modern cruisers. The Royal Navy had 225 destroyers, half of which were of modern design and the rest serviceable for escort duties. British submarine design had lagged behind that of France, Germany and Italy and although the navy could deploy 75, many were only suitable for harbour protection and coastal operations.

Manning this huge fleet was no problem, for in addition to the normal reserve system, Churchill (First Lord of the Admiralty since 1911) had created an 'Immediate Reserve' of men available prior to general mobilisation.

The Super-dreadnought, HMS *Queen Elizabeth*, under fire from the Turkish shore batteries at the entrance to the Dardanelles, 18 March 1915, during the ill-fated attempt of the Anglo-French fleet to force the Narrows at Chanak and fight its way into the Sea of Marmara and on to Constantinople. (Liddle Centre for World War 1)

Russian cruiser *Askold* in the Aegean, 1915. Her five funnels inevitably resulted in her being known to the British as 'The Packet of Woodbines.' Part of the Russian Black Sea Fleet, she had been cruising in the Mediterranean and Aegean as war broke out and was unable to regain her home port. Her main battery of 12 6-inch guns proved invaluable as fire support for the troops landed on the Gallipoli peninsula. (IWM)

In his years as 1st Sea Lord, Fisher had scrapped over 150 obsolete warships. As a result, on mobilisation, several thousand reserve officers and ratings were without seagoing berths. Formed into the Royal Naval Division and re-trained as infantry, they served initially in the futile defence of Antwerp in the autumn of 1914, then at Gallipoli, and finally on the Western Front.

Despite the Royal Navy's numerical superiority, there were some shortcomings. In the design of armour-piercing shells, moored mines and torpedoes Britain had lagged behind other naval powers. But in naval aviation, Britain was ahead. The world's first purpose-built aircraft carrier, *Ark Royal*, had joined the fleet and was to serve in the Mediterranean in support of the Dardanelles operations, and several capital ships had been modified to carry seaplanes.

The British Army of 1914 was not designed for prolonged continental war. The nation had traditionally relied for its security on the Royal Navy and the all-regular army was in fact a form of colonial *gendarmerie* whose primary role was imperial policing. Secret staff talks with the French general staff resulted in the formation of an expeditionary force, which was sent to join the French and Belgian armies at the outbreak of war. Apart from units brought back from the empire and colonies there were no more regulars and two sources of manpower had to be tapped: the Territorial Force, constitutionally tied to Home Defence (unless its members individually opted to serve overseas, which most did) and the 'New Army' of volunteers responding to Kitchener's recruiting campaign.

The regular army was highly disciplined, highly proficient in rifle shooting, and took

Men of the British 11th Infantry Division filling their water bottles at Suvla Bay, Gallipoli. One of the three 'Kitchener' divisions landed in August 1915, its commander, Major General Hammersley, suffered a nervous breakdown within days and had to be medically evacuated. These troops, trained and equipped to fight on the Western Front in static trench warfare conditions, were pitched into battle at Gallipoli at the height of summer. Lack of water led to hundreds of casualties from dehydration and heat stroke within days of their arrival. (IWM)

great pride in regimental traditions. Apart from four regiments of Foot Guards there were 69 infantry regiments of the line. Each had had several Territorial battalions, the successors to the Volunteers of the 19th century. At the outbreak of war Kitchener's assessment was that it would last far longer than Christmas 1914 and that there would be a grim requirement for what he realistically knew to be cannon-fodder. The best of the nation came forward in answer to his appeal. The first to see action would be landed at Gallipoli in August 1915; brave, enthusiastic, but inadequately trained and led, and bewildered by the task set for them.

As in most continental armies of 1914 the basic formation was the infantry division of some 18,000 men, comprising three brigades of four battalions. Each division was supported by its integral artillery: four brigades (equivalent to the modern gunner regiment) of three batteries. Three brigades were equipped with the 18-pounder QF (quick firing) gun and the fourth with the 4.5 inch howitzer. The cavalry division contained two brigades of horse artillery with the 13-pounder QF gun. All these guns were horse-drawn.

An infantry battalion at full war establishment had nearly 1,000 men. The primary weapon was the Lee-Enfield bolt-operated rifle whose magazine held 10 rounds of .303 inch ball cartridge ammunition. The infantryman was trained to fire 15 aimed rounds a minute at ranges up to 500 yards and the effect of a good battalion shooting at this rate was devastating.

Until the sweeping reforms of Haldane, War Minister from 1905, the British army lacked a properly constituted General Staff on the lines of that at the heart of the Prussian war machine. By 1914 the Staff College at Camberley had produced enough highly trained staff officers to dispatch the British Expeditionary Force to France and man its key staff appointments at all levels down to brigade headquarters, but thereafter the position worsened, particularly with regard to the rapidly expanding 'Kitchener Army'. This shortfall was evident when New Army units were put to the test at Gallipoli and on the Western Front.

The most technically proficient arms were the Royal Artillery and Royal Engineers. The artillery was organised into three branches, Horse, Field and Garrison. The Royal Horse Artillery was regarded as an *elite*, descended from the galloping batteries devised to outshoot Napoleon's field artillery and move tactically at the speed of the cavalry. Heavier artillery weapons like the 60-pounder were manned by the Royal Garrison Artillery who also, as the name implied, operated static weapons in fortresses and the semi-mobile long-range guns that progressively joined the order of battle in all theatres. Logistics were provided for the field army by the Army Service and Ordnance Corps, which between them dealt with the provision, storage and distribution of all supplies and warlike stores, transport, and repair services. The Royal Army Medical Corps greatly increased in size on mobilisation by enlisting the services of a reserve to which hundreds of the country's leading consultants belonged, having carried out a prescribed amount of military medical training each year.

Italy

Prior to Italian unification in the second half of the 19th century armies had been raised by various states up and down the peninsula. None of these was strong enough to stand by itself against more powerful neighbours and as a result Italy was ruled for centuries by Austria under the Habsburgs in the north and by Bourbon Spain in the south. The Papal states managed to retain a degree of autonomy, as did the Piedmontese, who had a strong military tradition. By 1866 guerrilla warfare led by Garibaldi culminated in the proclamation of the United Kingdom of Italy which, allied with Prussia against Austria, extended its territory by acquisition of the Venetian provinces. Austria's desire to recover these would be a primary excuse for her bellicose attitudes in the period leading to war in 1914. The army of Savoy saw service in the Crimea and some of its regiments, like the Bersaglieri and Alpini, were famed throughout Europe. The emergence of a truly national army was slow, for the northerners looked down on Garibaldi's irregulars and Neapolitans. There was little public enthusiasm for conscription, introduced after 1861. When sent in to repress civil unrest, the army did so robustly. It became a folk tradition for young men in the south to evade military service by taking to the hills at call-up time.

By 1910 conscription had become acceptable although about 20 per cent of the population successfully dodged their military service. The army liked to think of itself as the school of the nation in the old Prussian manner, but its Ethiopian campaign of 1896 was disastrous; hundreds of Italian soldiers taken prisoner were murdered or castrated. The army redeemed its name by beating the Turks in Libya in 1911–12, deploying nearly 100,000 troops to Tripolitania and Cyrenaica. As a result, the army was short of virtually every sort of munition and armament in 1914. There were still four classes of conscript serving with the colours (as opposed to the normal two) but from a peacetime strength of 14,000 officers and 852,000 soldiers the army on mobilisation in May 1915, even with the recall of older classes of reservists, could raise and equip only 35 divisions and was short of artillery and ammunition reserves. For this reason Italy's entry into the war was delayed until General Cadorna, the Chief of Staff, was satisfied that the army was fully ready. By

A 60-pounder gun of the Royal Garrison Artillery in action at Cape Helles, Gallipoli. A chronic shortage of field artillery and ammunition severely inhibited the performance of British troops throughout this ill-starred campaign. By August 1915 most of the 60-pounders had broken down and lack of spares had reduced their number to a single gun. (IWM)

1917 he was commanding 67 divisions in the field, despite appalling casualties as the result of his bovine assaults against the near-impregnable Austrian defences on the Isonzo front.

Serbia

The Serbian military system demanded universal service for all able-bodied males from the age of 18 to 45. The army conspicuously lacked motorised transport, due in part to the appalling standard of Serbian roads, generally impassable to motors after rain. The army's transportation relied on animals. Baggage trains, bridging equipment and artillery were all drawn by oxen. Country wagons hauled by two or four animals were the usual method of carrying supplies. The strength of the Serbian army lay in the endurance and courage of its officers and soldiers, who displayed amazing powers of survival in their campaigns. In peacetime the army comprised five active divisions, each of which had its own reserve division; thus the mobilised strength was 10 self-contained divisions, a 'bayonet strength' of some 180,000.

Austria-Hungary

The Austrian army was strong on tradition, many of its regiments claiming descent from those that had fought the Turks in the

17th century (the *Hoch-und-Deutschmeister* regiment, founded by the Teutonic knights in 1696, claimed an even more venerable ancestry as the military wing of an order founded in the 12th century). With the steady expansion of the empire, however, it had been necessary to recruit increasingly from non-German elements. Problems of loyalty and language arose as German-speaking units became outnumbered by the other ethnic groups. By 1914 less than 30 per cent of the army was Germanic. Germans, Hungarians and Czechs, being the better educated, went into the artillery, engineers and cavalry. Almost 70 per cent of men in the so-called Common Infantry

regiments were Slavs. Magyars hated Slavs, and care had to be taken in mixing their formations. Language was a major problem, tackled by using a universal *patois* known as 'Army Slav' in addition to which recruits were required to learn up to 80 German words of command.

Manning was a huge problem in peacetime. In 1910, out of the empire's total population of some 50 million, only 125,000 were available for conscription. The army's peace establishment was under 500,000, expanding on full mobilisation to 3,350,000. This included various second-line categories such as *Landwehr*, *Landsturm*, *Ersatz* reserve and, in Hungary, the *Honved*. In theory every fit man from the age of 19 was liable for conscription, serving an initial two years with the colours before entering the reserve system.

Serbian artillery on the move – the guns were normally drawn by oxen, as the roads were of poor quality and usually impassable to motor vehicles. (IWM)

Germany

Germany's chief preoccupations were the Western and Eastern Fronts, but there was a recurrent need to bail the Austrians and Turks out of trouble, whether in the Balkans, in the Near East or, once Italy had entered the war, along the Austro-Italian border.

The German military tradition created by Frederick I of Prussia was crisply expressed in a letter he wrote to his son, the future Frederick the Great: 'Have money and a good army'. This philosophy created an unbroken succession of prodigiously professional generals – the younger Frederick, Scharnhorst, Gneisenau, Blücher, von Moltke the elder, down to the formidable duo Hindenburg and Ludendorff, and experts like Falkenhayn and von der Goltz, sent to all corners during the 1914–18 war to redeem predicaments in which their lesser allies had landed themselves. The professional officer class of the German army stemmed from the Junkers (lower gentry) of Prussia; poor, patriotic, Protestant and proud. But some of the pre-unification armies managed to survive alongside the Prussian, including those of Bavaria, Hanover, Saxony, Brunswick, Mecklenburg, Wurttemburg and Hesse, some retaining traditions dating back to their service under the English and Hanoverian crowns. All were embraced by the Prussian system after unification, apart from those that had fought on the losing Austrian side against Prussia in the war of 1866.

The Prussian officer caste set the tone for German social life. It was considered an honour to 'wear the King's coat' of Prussian blue. The true *elite*, however, were the graduates of the Prussian *Kriegsakademie* founded in 1811, nursery of the General Staff, who were responsible for intricate mobilisation and deployment planning and for the strategic direction of the German war machine. They had long worked on the assumption that Germany might have to fight a war on two fronts; against Russia in the east and France and her Allies in the west. Schlieffen based his plans on a quick knockout blow against the French army, which he knew could quadruple its peace strength in a few days with a mobilisation system as efficient as the German. He would then use a highly effective railway network to shift the main body of the army to East Prussia to dispose of the Russians, who mobilised more slowly.

The Prussian system relied on conscription. At the age of 17 young men entered the *Landsturm* for preliminary part-time training at regimental depots close to their homes. They entered two or three years' service with the colours at the age of 20 before going into the reserve, liable for call-out up to the age of 45. Older reservists were required to serve in units for home defence or lines of communication duties.

The core formation, the infantry division of about 18,000 men, comprised infantry, machine gun, artillery, cavalry and engineer units supported by medical, signal and supply columns. The cavalry division consisted of mounted regiments and horse artillery, totalling some 6,000 men. The German organisational model was generally followed by all the European powers. As the war progressed it was found by most of the combatant nations that infantry battalions over 1,000 strong were too cumbersome and the establishments were pruned, yielding surplus manpower for the raising of additional units.

A German infantry division comprised two brigades, each of two regiments of three battalions. Active (ie Regular) and Reserve Army Corps consisted of two divisions. The division's artillery comprised 12 six-gun batteries; a total of 54 field guns (77 mm) and 18 light howitzers (105 mm). Heavier artillery units existed at Army corps level. Units of the German army involved in the Mediterranean theatre were gathered together specifically for participation in certain operations, notably on the Italian front, where *Jaeger* (light infantry), and mountain units served; in addition, as the war proceeded, specialist assault units, skilled in fast movement and fieldcraft, were used for the penetration of hostile defences, a technique which reached its peak in 1917 at Caporetto against the Italians and in 1918 against the British 5th Army on the Western Front.

Turkey

The Turkish army had been defeated by four small Balkan states in the three years prior to the outbreak of war in 1914. Despite this it was to fight doggedly until its final defeats in 1918. Much of the credit for its performance was due to the training teams of Germans under General Otto Liman von Sanders (active in Turkey from 1913) and the drastic reforms carried through by Enver Pasha the War Minister on their advice. Elderly time-serving officers were replaced by young, well-educated men from the Turkish middle classes. The German instructors had faced serious problems, apart from the conservatism and national pride of Turkish officers who resented their presence. There was a shortage of manpower, and communications in Asia Minor were appallingly bad. The Turkish population in 1914 was about 19 million in the core provinces, and perhaps another six million in outlying ones where non-Muslim populations paid higher tax in lieu of military service. Muslims could also evade service and the prosperous, better-educated urban classes tended to escape the draft in this way. In wartime, units of poor Christian Greeks and Armenians, regarded as untrustworthy in the line, were assigned to fatigue duties; the fighting cadre of the army was the Anatolian peasant soldier; patriotic, generally ill-educated, brave, devout and enduring. About 100,000 young men were liable for call-up each year but administrative incompetence meant that only 75 per cent of these actually reached the training depots. The peacetime strength of the army was some 250,000, comprising two years' call-up classes. On mobilisation, numbers rose to 800,000 but this took up to six months to achieve. In France and Germany some 10 per cent of the population could be conscripted; the figure for Turkey was less than half this.

Turkish conscripts were liable to a total of 17 years active and reserve service with the navy, 25 years in the infantry, or 20 in the technical arms like the engineers and artillery. Of these, naval conscripts served five years full time (*nizam*) in the navy, two

in the infantry and three in the technical troops, before passing into successive grades of reserve or *Redif*. At the end of the reserve obligation there was still the territorial force, a militia known as the *Musathfiz*, an obligation so tenuous that there was not even a peacetime cadre. The *Jandarma*, a paramilitary internal security force, was recruited from reliable ex-regular and conscript soldiers.

The reformed Ottoman army of 1915 was grouped in four regional armies, based in Constantinople, Baghdad, Erzerum and Erzinjan. A further five armies were created during the war, and the pre-mobilisation strength of 36 divisions increased to 70 by 1917. Army corps were formed by pairing a *redif* division with a *nizam reserve*; even so, few divisions or army corps ever reached their full war establishment. A division consisted of three regiments, each of three battalions. The artillery branch was historically independent, enjoying an elite status stemming back to the days of Mehmet II, conqueror of Constantinople in 1453 and the world's first great artillery commander. The standard field gun was the Krupp 75 mm, but a wide assortment of elderly pieces were in service; the large calibre fortress guns, like those installed in the defences of the Dardanelles, were mostly obsolete and short of suitable ammunition. But some of the batteries closer to the Chanak Narrows were equipped with relatively modern Krupp and Schneider-Creusot 150 mm howitzers dating from the 1890s.

On the basis of scanty intelligence assessments of the Turkish army's equipment and the perceived incompetence of much of its officer class the British and French seriously underestimated their opponent; the true strength of the Turks lay in their ordinary soldiers and the patriotism that inspired them to defend their native soil.

France

French military organisation followed the German pattern in many respects. An army

corps consisted of two divisions, each of two brigades of three battalions apiece. All formations from brigade upwards enjoyed the services of integrated support troops; the field artillery was equipped with what was probably the outstanding gun of its type in any army at that time: the 75 mm *Soixante-Quinze*, capable of loosing off 20 rounds a minute. The army included both metropolitan and colonial units. French troops engaged at the Dardanelles and Salonika included Metropolitan battalions,

A Rolls Royce armoured car of the Duke of Westminster's squadron at Sollum, April 1916. In the second World War, deep penetration patrols of the Long Range Desert Group were baffled when they came across wheel tracks left in the hard sand of the Qattara Depression by the Westminster cars almost 30 years previously. After the conclusion of operations against the Senussi the cars were transferred to Palestine where they operated closely with Allenby's mounted troops in the concluding battles of that campaign. (IWM)

African Zouaves, Annamese and Foreign Legion units.

Greece

The ambivalent position of Greece in the First World War stemmed from the polarity between Prime Minister Eleftherios Venizelos and King Constantine, exacerbated by chronic political turbulence. In 1833, independence had been secured by a raggle-taggle army of idealistic irregulars, foreign Hellenists and unashamed bandit gangs. The first King of the Hellenes, Otto, brought with him 3,500 fellow Bavarians as the unpopular cadre of a 'national' army. Only a few Greeks were allowed to serve, as garrison troops in Athens, and these mutinied in 1843 to secure the Hellenisation of the entire army. When Otto was deposed in 1863 the army had been developed on Germanic lines. In the next reign, that of a Danish prince, the bond between throne and army was strengthened and Crown Prince Constantine, who ably commanded in the field in the Balkan Wars of 1912–13, was a graduate of the Prussian Staff College. By 1914 he was king, favouring the cause of the Central Powers and hoping devoutly for their victory.

Prime Minister Venizelos was a rabid Greek nationalist, infused by what became known in 19th century Greece as the 'Great Idea'. Recalling the glories of ancient Greece, it visualised the annexation of all areas of south west Europe with Greek-speaking populations plus Crete and Cyprus, Constantinople and parts of western Anatolia. The idea was enthusiastically taken up by the Greek intelligentsia and the army became steadily more and more politicised. When international pressure in 1909

Minesweeping operations in the Dardanelles. The destroyer HMS *Racoon*, hit by fire from shore batteries, blows off steam as another destroyer closes with her to take her on tow; a battleship – either *Agamemnon* or *Lord Nelson*, provides cover. In the far distance, aground at Sedd-el-Bahr, can be seen the collier *River Clyde* used as the 'Trojan Horse' for the landings on 25 April. (IWM)

A French 75 mm Quick-Firer – the celebrated
'Soixante-Quinze' – in action at Helles, Gallipoli, during
an attempt to take Krithia. This gun is at full recoil. An
extremely high rate of fire of up to 20 rounds a minute
was possible. The French at Gallipoli, unlike the British,
were not inhibited by ammunition shortage for their field
artillery and were able to give invaluable fire support to
their allies' assaults that otherwise have proved even
more costly than was the case. (IWM)

compelled the Greek government
temporarily to shelve the idea of annexing
Crete, the army revolted and Venizelos,
himself a Cretan, became prime minister. In
1915, as his King and many of the senior
generals backed a German victory, he openly
declared for the Anglo-French alliance,
seeing this as a chance to be rewarded in due
course with a large slice of Turkish Anatolia.
Deposed by the King, Venizelos set up a
government in exile on Crete until the Allies
acted to disarm the royalist army and forced
Constantine to resign in 1916. The Greek
army, purged of most of its senior officers,
then took the field on the Allied side.

Countdown to war

By 1910 Germany and Britain, formerly good friends tied by a common royal house, had become estranged. Thwarted German colonial ambition, anxiety in Britain over the growth of the Imperial German Navy, a burning desire for revenge by France for its humiliations in 1871, combined with the serpentine politics and vendettas of the Balkans to create the right conditions for detonation. The spark came with the assassination of the heir to the Austrian throne at Sarajevo in June 1914. Nothing could have been more pleasing to Conrad, the Austrian Chief of Staff. He sought the elimination of Serbia as a prerequisite for embarking on more perilous military adventures against Italy and Russia. It was widely put about in Austria that the archduke's murder was a Serbian plot. The assassin, Gavrilo Princip, was a Serb student and member of a Serbian secret society, but there was little to prove that he was acting for his country's government. Nevertheless, hotheads in the Austrian government insisted on presenting Serbia with an unacceptable ultimatum on 23 July 1914, requiring an answer within 48 hours. It was drafted by Count Berchtold who believed, with his friend Conrad the Chief of Staff, that the time was ripe to crush Serbia and thus clear the route for the Berlin-Baghdad railway.

The Serbs began to mobilise, calling on the Russians for help. The German ambassadors in London, Paris and St Petersburg insisted that Austria's demands were perfectly 'moderate and fair', and the Kaiser continued with his summer holiday on the imperial yacht after visiting Kiel Regatta where German and British naval officers enjoyed a last week of socialising before war made them enemies. In Constantinople the German battlecruiser *Goeben* and her escorting cruiser *Breslau* had been anchored ostentatiously off the German embassy in the Bosphorus over the summer, greatly admired by the populace. Now, the ships quietly slipped away to a secret assignment. The Turkish people awaited the arrival from England of two prestigious additions to their navy: two super-dreadnoughts purchased largely by public subscription, whose crews had already gone to Tyneside to collect them.

Serbia's mobilisation was completed by the end of July and the government left Belgrade for its alternative location at Nis as the Austrians massed along the frontier. On mobilisation it was revealed that there were only 500 rounds for each Austrian field gun. Conrad faced war on two fronts as the Russians mobilised and deployed on the northern border, with the threat that they would invade Austria if Serbian territory were violated. In Berlin, General Helmuth von Moltke, Chief of the General Staff, drafted an ultimatum to Belgium demanding free and unopposed passage for the German army as it delivered its right hook against France. It was handed to the German ambassador in Brussels for presentation when ordered.

On 27 July the Austrian cabinet decided to declare war on Serbia next day. A weeping emperor, who had advised caution throughout, signed the declaration. When Francis Joseph read the Serbian response to the Austrian ultimatum he decided that there were no longer grounds for war; but by then it was far too late. By 30 July diplomatic telegrams were flying in all directions as Kings, Presidents and Tsars frantically tried to arrest the slide into war; but the inexorable machinery of general mobilisation, once started, could not be stopped. On 1 August Germany declared war on Russia and in Britain the two Turkish battleships *Sultan Osman I* and *Reshadieh* were taken into the

Royal Navy as HMS *Agincourt* and *Erin* on the pretext that they could have been used in the German fleet. There was outrage in Turkey and this act of *realpolitik* played a major part in Turkey's subsequent entry into the war on the side of the Central Powers. On 2 August the German ultimatum was presented to the Belgians as Turkey signed a secret pact with Germany to ensure mutual defence against Russia. The Serbs stood by to defend their country, having assembled some 485,000 men in only six days. On 3 August Germany and France were at war, and late on the following evening Britain declared war on Germany.

War in the Mediterranean

The strategies adopted in the Mediterranean campaigns were governed by geographical as well as by political factors. The Central Powers enjoyed few outlets to the open seas. Germany's were effectively closed from the start by the presence of the British Grand Fleet at Scapa Flow and the North Sea and Channel ports. Austria's navy, though not insignificant, was based on the Adriatic, which could be closed across the Straits of Otranto by a hostile fleet. In 1914 it was unprepared for major operations and was kept at Pola, its main base. Turkey's navy, comprising mostly ancient ships until the acquisition of the powerful former German warships *Goeben* and *Breslau*, could readily be

confined within the Dardanelles by an Allied blockading fleet based on adjacent Greek islands. Italy had an extensive coastline on the Adriatic and Mediterranean and following her entry into the war in 1915 her fleet's main preoccupation was the neutralisation of the Austrian Adriatic fleet. The French Mediterranean fleet's planned war role had been to confront the Austrian and Italian fleets, but as the Austrians were shut in the Adriatic and the Italians failed to

The dummy 'battlecruiser' *Tiger*, constructed on a merchant ship. The ruse worked, and the U-boat commander who sank her was aghast to see her funnel, tripod mast and guns floating away in the eastern Mediterranean as she went down. (IWM)

Summer 1915. A scene at Mudros Harbour, the main allied naval base on the island of Lemnos. Numerous merchant ships and a light cruiser are at anchor, and a naval dirigible airship patrols overhead. In the foreground, two steam pinnaces act as safety boats for a bathing parade from a warship – probably one of the pre-dreadnought battleships – whose anti-torpedo netting is visible in the left-hand corner. (IWM)

join the Central Powers in the Triple Alliance it found itself contributing to the Allied blockade of the Dardanelles.

British strategic interests centred on the Suez Canal, the route to India. Turkey's entry into the war on the side of the Central Powers was not unexpected, (though it might have been avoided had the British government matched the Germans in their diplomatic handling of the Sublime Porte in the years before the war). Turkey's closure of the Dardanelles cut Russia off from her western Allies, preventing the export of Ukrainian grain and oil that would have financed her war effort. It also denied the Allies the ability to supply Russia with munitions and weapons. Strategically, Turkey's entry threatened the Suez Canal and

Russian territory in the Caucasus. The proclamation of *jihad* by the Sultan/Caliph on the outbreak of war seemed to pose a threat to the structure of the Indian Army and its Muslim soldiers. Although this danger did not materialise it inhibited the use of these valuable regiments against soldiers of their own faith. The threat posed to India by Russia had largely evaporated since 1904, but a significant garrison still had to be maintained in India on the north-west frontier and for internal security. The Persian Gulf assumed a new strategic significance with the development of oil fields, largely under Anglo-French control, on the fringe of the Ottoman Empire. This oil was essential to the fuelling of the battle fleets, which were then changing over from coal to oil fuel. The threat of German influence in this area via the Berlin-Baghdad railway, even though this was still incomplete, necessitated an expeditionary force from India to secure the oilfields and advance up the Tigris and Euphrates rivers. As if these problems were not enough, the British C-in-C Egypt had to face the threat of insurrection in his rear.

Immediately before the outbreak of war in August 1914 two dreadnoughts, destined for the Imperial Ottoman Navy, were fitting out on the Tyne and their crews were preparing to sail them home to Constantinople. Instead, they were taken over, on Winston Churchill's orders, and became HMS *Agincourt* and *Erin* in the Grand Fleet. Both were to serve at the battle of Jutland in 1916. There was widespread dismay and resentment in Turkey, where the population had contributed on a nation-wide basis for their purchase, and this was a major factor towards Turkey's entry into the war on the side of the Central Powers. Here HMS *Agincourt* is seen at the time of the British takeover. (IWM)

Enver Pasha, encouraged by the Germans, was stirring up the dissident tribes of Libya, where the Italians had supplanted the Turks in 1912, but now found the subjects of the Grand Senussi of Sollum agitated by the proclamation of Holy War against the infidel.

The Mediterranean war can be said to have started on the day the French declared war, when the two German warships on the loose in the western Mediterranean materialised off the north African coast and bombarded two ports. But it was on the Serbian border that the serious fighting began.

Invasion of Serbia

Serbia's geographical position made it the strategic keystone of the Balkan peninsula. The terrain was wild and mountainous but two historic Balkan trade routes passed through it along the Morava–Maritza Trench, known as the 'Diagonal Furrow' (the line selected for the Berlin–Baghdad railway), and the Morava–Vardar Trench, connecting Central Europe with the Aegean. Serbia's northern frontier was shielded by natural barriers, the rivers Drina and Danube. Neither was fordable and in 1914 the only bridge over the Danube in Serbia was at Belgrade. A third barrier, the river Sava, was lined with near-impassable marshes. Road communication throughout the country was extremely poor. The population consisted mostly of hardy peasant farmers.

The Serbs began to mobilise on 26 July 1914. The Austrian Chief of Staff, Conrad, was discovering that despite his haste to go to war, the army was ill-prepared for active service. He also had to deploy eight army corps to the Russian border. Despite this Austria declared war on Serbia on 28 July. A day later, Austrian warships on the Danube bombarded Belgrade as their 2nd, 4th and 6th armies under General Oskar Potiorek prepared to cross the rivers Sava and Drina. The Serbs, with 450,000 men supported by partly trained Montenegrins, all under command of Marshal Radomir Putnik, resolved to sell their lives dearly. Putnik, with some 450 miles of frontier with Austria and Bulgaria to defend, deployed his three armies centrally to meet threats from either direction. He aimed to hold the key river lines with small formations then, having located the main crossings, to attack them in strength on ground of his own choice. He

correctly forecast the Austrians' main thrust lines and was ready when they came. Potiorek's approach was hesitant and many of his ill-trained troops were unwilling to fight fellow Slavs. There was much indiscipline in the ranks and horrific atrocities were committed by Austrian units against Serbian civilians.

Battle was joined in earnest on 12 August when, in nine days of ferocious fighting, the Serbs threw the Austrians back across their start lines in the battle of Jadar and advanced into Bosnia in hot pursuit. The Austrians fled in disorder. On 7 September Potiorek tried again, forcing the over-extended Serbs back out of Bosnia. By early November it seemed that all was up,

but at that point the frail and elderly King Peter, carrying a private soldier's rifle, entered the trenches with his sons, inspiring his troops with the words:

Heroes – you have taken two oaths: one to me, your King, and the other to your country. I am an old broken man on the edge of the grave and I release you from your oath to me. From your other oath no one can release you. If you feel you cannot go on, go to your homes, and I pledge my word that after the war, if we come out of it, nothing shall happen to you. But I and my sons stay here.

Not a man left the line. Sheer weight of numbers forced the Serbs to evacuate Belgrade on 29 November but on 3 December Putnik,

having completed a withdrawal in good order to the south west, turned and counter-attacked on the line of the Kolubara river, King Peter still in the front line with his rifle and 50 rounds of ammunition. The Austrians again fled in confusion. By the 15 December Serbian patrols were back in Belgrade where the King attended a solemn *Te Deum* in the cathedral. The third Austrian invasion had collapsed ignominiously with the loss of 41,000 prisoners and 133 guns. Potiorek was replaced by the Archduke Eugene.

The Serbian front now went quiet as the Austrians endeavoured to cope with the alarming situation on their Russian front. In response to Serbian appeals, Admiral Troubridge of the British Mediterranean fleet, eccentrically clad in the uniform of a Serbian general to confound German intelligence, arrived in Belgrade in February 1915 with a naval detachment including eight 4.7 inch guns for the city's defence. Meanwhile typhus was decimating the Serb army; by April 48,000 soldiers were in hospital. The summer of 1915 saw little more than skirmishing as the Serbs built up their strength for what they realised would be a hard winter. Germany was desperate to reopen the Berlin-Baghdad rail link and could not do so until Serbia was conquered. The Austrians, appalled by their losses to date and unwilling to tackle the Serbs on their own, looked to Bulgaria, whose government was sitting on the fence. There was a hint that they would consider joining Britain and France if given large tracts of land including Serbian and Greek Macedonia. Eventually German patience ran out; on 6 September 1915 a convention was signed between Germany, Austria and Bulgaria, aimed at crushing Serbian resistance. The Allies, alarmed, made a final unconditional offer to Bulgaria of part of Macedonia. It was

The Headquarters of the 29th Division, overlooking Gully Beach, Helles, summer 1915. Concealed from the view of Turkish observers and to some extent shielded from enemy artillery fire, this was an almost idyllic spot on an otherwise unpleasant part of the front. Staff officers' memoirs recall their delight at sitting on their terraced hillside, drinking whisky as the sun went down behind the island of Samothrace. (IWM)

turned down, and Serbia's fate was sealed. German forces joined the Austrians on the northern border and the Allies belatedly realised that they had lost a major diplomatic battle by not insisting that the Greeks fulfilled the treaty terms binding them to help Serbia. On 22 September a French mission arrived at Salonika to assess its suitability as a base for the support of the Serbs. In an effort to involve the Greeks, Serbia offered them territory on the border. Constantine reluctantly gave permission for Allied troops to land at Salonika as his prime minister made a vain last-ditch appeal for the Bulgars to suspend mobilisation if the Greeks did likewise. It was too late; the die had been cast.

The Austro-German forces massing on the northern frontier were commanded by Field Marshal August von Mackensen, fresh from his crushing defeat of the Russians at Gorlice-Tarnow. Charged with the total defeat of the Serbs he headed a joint force including the newly mobilised Bulgarians.

On 5 October a huge artillery bombardment began the offensive. Next day Belgrade came under attack and the British naval gunners fought to the end as the capital fell on the 9th after savage street fighting costing the Austrians 7,000 casualties. The balance had tipped in favour of the Central Powers, and the great fortress of Mitrovitza fell to the Austrians on 23 November as the Serbs withdrew south and west. On the same day the Bulgars linked hands with General von Gallwitz's German troops. The Bulgarian advance had cut the Serbs off from the Anglo-French force now established in its bridgehead around Salonika, from which it had earlier been possible to supply Putnik's army.

The Serb retirement continued. Morale was still high, men were flocking in to enlist, and the fighting qualities of the Serb army remained as strong as ever; but they were steadily forced to give ground and the great arsenal of Kragujevac was abandoned and blown up on 1 November. The army retreated onto the Kossovo Plain as the new seat of government was set up at Mitrovica. On 16 November, as winter closed in, the city of

The aged King Peter I of Serbia being lifted into his saddle by his staff. Born in 1844 into the ruling Karageorgevic family, he had fought in the French army in its war of 1870–71 and became king in 1903 by election. Fiercely patriotic, he insisted on going into the field with the Serb army in 1914 despite his age and infirmity and accompanied his men on their terrible march across the mountains into exile in Greece. In 1918 he returned to his homeland as King of the Serbs, Croats and Slovenes, albeit under the regency of his son Alexander. (IWM)

Monastir fell; the army was now in dire straits, its last links with Greece cut, typhus raging, all troops on half rations and only 200 field guns left. As Mitrovica and Pristina fell on 23 November the surviving 200,000 Serbian troops faced a nightmare march over mountains in the grip of winter, to safety on the Adriatic coast. The Serbian rearguard was overwhelmed on the White Drin river, losing masses of precious supplies in the process as the retreat went on in dreadful weather. A new seat of government and General Headquarters were established at Scutari on the Albanian coast as the Allies rushed shipping into the Adriatic to embark the battered survivors.

A French force that had belatedly set out from Salonika up the Vardar valley to help the Serbs was met by overwhelming Bulgarian forces and compelled to fall back in some disorder with a British division, the 10th (Irish), shielding its left flank. The Allies withdrew to a defended line, the so-called 'Entrenched Camp', some 14 miles inland from Salonika itself, where they remained for the rest of the winter. It had not been an auspicious start. The Greek King was informed that the surviving Serbs were going to the island of Corfu, already occupied by French marines without the Greeks' permission; the transfer began on 12 January 1916 as the Salonika garrison blew the bridge over the River Struma in the presence of indignant Greek troops. The Salonika campaign had got under way.

The Mesopotamian sideshow

The British government had already appreciated the vulnerability of strategic oil

supplies from the Persian Gulf. It was decided that military operations in that area should be directed from India, under political control of the India and Colonial Offices in London. Initially there was no input from the War Office as the troops involved were from the Indian Army. This split command system led to confusion and near-disaster. A small force was dispatched from India in September 1914 to secure the Anglo-Persian Oil Company's installations at Abadan and the pipe-head from the up-country oilfields, and to ensure the continuing loyalty of the various sheikhdoms along the Gulf in view of the *jihad* proclaimed in Constantinople. With the initial objectives secured, more troops were sent from India to implement the second phase of the operation, an advance up the Shatt-el-Arab to Basra, which was entered on 22 November.

After further reinforcements had arrived from India the force pushed up the Tigris and Euphrates rivers, supplied by a small armada of steamers and towed barges. Two infantry divisions and a cavalry brigade made up an improvised army corps under General Sir John Nixon of the Indian Army. As the Turks resisted vigorously along the Euphrates a second force under Major General Townshend advanced up the less heavily defended Tigris. Townshend drove his men hard through the blazing summer of 1915. In September he reached Ctesiphon, only 22 miles from Baghdad. Short of rations, weary and low-spirited, his Indian

The Mesopotamian theatre, 1914–17

Mosul

PERSIA

Baghdad
Ctesiphon
Kut-al-Amara
Sannavat

Tigris

Nasiriyah
Euphrates
Oil fields

ARABIAN DESERT   Basra
Pipe line
Abadan

N

KUWAIT

PERSIAN
GULF

0   100 miles
0   200 km

which time the defenders were on starvation rations, also failed and Townshend was given authority to negotiate a surrender. Some supplies were now reaching him, dropped from machines of the Royal Flying Corps, but the quantities were insufficient. Meanwhile von der Goltz died in Baghdad, probably of cholera (though some thought he was poisoned by a cabal of Young Turks). Khalil Pasha, the Turkish commander at Kut, assured Townshend that were he to capitulate, 'your gallant troops will be our most sincere and precious guests'. The subsequent treatment of Townshend's rank and file was appalling; he was escorted to Constantinople and regally treated but his men were subjected to a brutal 1,200 mile forced march to Anatolia on short rations, in the course of which over 4,000 died.

In August 1916 the arrival of General Sir Frederick Maude as commander-in-chief transformed the campaign. Control passed to the War Office in London. Maude insisted on massive reinforcements and the establishment of an efficient logistics system before resuming the offensive, which he did in December 1916. The Turks, though still fighting stubbornly, were racked by disease; their supply system was inefficient and they failed to stem Maude's relentless advance. He re-took Kut in February 1917 and entered Baghdad in triumph on 11 March, only to die there of cholera in October, in the same house in which von der Goltz had died.

Although Maude had a four-to-one numerical superiority over the Turks (who had barely 42,000 men) his army had overcome severe physical and psychological difficulties following Townshend's humiliation, and although the Dardanelles and Palestine campaigns were to create far more news and still retain an aura of glamour, he had successfully destroyed a main Turkish army. After the capture of Baghdad the urgency went out of the campaign; in any case the Russians were all but finished by the end of 1917 and Turkey was now so weakened that her armies no longer posed a serious threat to the Allies outside Palestine.

troops failed in a mishandled attack on 22 November. The Tigris was running low and the river steamers were unable to support the force, so Townshend fell back on Kut and dug a strong defensive position in a loop of the river, confident that he could sit it out until reinforcements of men and material reached him when the river returned to its winter flow. The Turks, now under the command of the former adviser to the Sultan, General (Field Marshal in the Ottoman army) Colmar von der Goltz, closely invested the garrison. A number of attempts to rescue Townshend failed ignominiously. By January 1916 supplies were running low and the garrison slaughtered their horses for food, an idea repulsive to most of the Indian troops. A final overland relief attempt on 16 April, by

Gallipoli and the Dardanelles

The campaign in the Dardanelles and on the Gallipoli peninsula was one of the most intriguing and tragic of the war. On 2 January 1915 the Russians appealed for some sort of demonstration by the Allies that would divert attention from the Caucasus, where the Tsar's troops were facing an ill-conceived Turkish offensive mounted, against the advice of his German Allies, by Enver Pasha the War Minister.

For some time Winston Churchill had tried to persuade his colleagues in Prime Minister Asquith's Cabinet to adopt a strategy of indirect approach to resolve the deadlock on the Western Front. Churchill's idea was to force the Dardanelles, seize Constantinople and by knocking Turkey out of the war, undermine the entire strategy of the Central Powers. Kitchener was reluctant to divert any effort from the west, and was supported by the General Staff and Field Marshal Sir John French,

Aristocrats on active service with the 10th (Irish) Division at Suvla, Gallipoli, August 1915: Captain The Marquess of Headfort, ADC to Lt General Sir Bryan Mahon; Lt Colonel the Earl of Granard, PC, commanding 5th (pioneer) battalion Royal Irish Regiment and Lord Granard, as a Privy Counsellor, took it upon himself to write personally to the King, drawing attention to the inept handling of the campaign at Suvla Bay. When General Sir Ian Hamilton was told of this he administered a courteous reproof to Granard. (IWM)

commander of the British Expeditionary Force, who believed that it was only in France that the German main army could be beaten and the war won. Faced with Kitchener's refusal to allocate ground forces for an expedition, Churchill sought and obtained sanction to mount a purely naval attack. His 1st Sea Lord, 'Jacky' Fisher, immediately raised objections; he had seen the Dardanelles defences for himself in 1878 and was convinced that their guns could still inflict catastrophic damage to any battle fleet trying to negotiate the Chanak Narrows. Once in the Sea of Marmara, the

A seaplane of the Royal Naval Air Service (RNAS) at Mudros harbour, Lemnos, during the Dardanelles operations. Lord Kitchener had specifically ruled out the use of the Royal Flying Corps at Gallipoli but the Royal Naval Air Service, using a miscellany of primitive aircraft, carried out reconnaissance, spotting for the guns of the fleet, photographic sorties and before long, torpedo bombing of any Turkish ships that could be found in the Sea of Marmara. As better aircraft became available the war was carried to Turkey's ally Bulgaria with some daring bombing attacks on the strategic railway linking Sofia with Constantinople. (IWM)

fleet would still require servicing by its oilers, colliers, victualling and ammunition ships and these, being unarmoured, would not stand a chance of survival at the close ranges involved. As it was, Fisher had declined to allot any modern battleships to the Anglo-French fleet blockading the Straits. A desultory bombardment was opened on the outer forts on 19 February 1915, surrendering any advantage of surprise.

As early as 13 December 1914 the British submarine B-11 had torpedoed the ancient Turkish battleship *Messudieh* off the town of Chanak; before long, British and French submarines were braving mines and submarine nets to enter the Sea of Marmara,

there to cause chaos to Turkish maritime trade. In February and March 1915 landing parties went ashore to complete the destruction of the outer forts on the European and Asiatic shores of the entry to the Straits. On German advice the Turks improved their defences against the expected Allied attack, deploying mobile howitzers on both sides of the Straits. Early in March Vice Admiral Carden, the fleet commander, announced he was ready to launch the naval attack on the Narrows, timed for the 18th. Meanwhile in London, Churchill's persistence had secured the use of ground troops, who would land after a successful naval operation to secure the forts and batteries. The Australian Imperial Force (AIF) and several thousand New Zealanders had reached Alexandria *en route* to Britain and the Western Front. Formed into the Australian and New Zealand Army Corps (Anzac) under Lieutenant General Sir William Birdwood of the Indian Army, they were retained in Egypt, ostensibly for further training and the defence of the Suez Canal. Another force available to Churchill was the Royal Naval Division (RND). Its battalions were made up of naval reservists and the

Royal Marine Light Infantry, mainly enthusiastic men who had responded to Kitchener's call for volunteers on the outbreak of war.

Early in March 1915 Kitchener appointed General Sir Ian Hamilton to command the Mediterranean Expeditionary Force (MEF). He received only the sketchiest of briefings from Kitchener before leaving London on 13 March, accompanied by a few staff officers, and with only meagre intelligence on the defences of the Dardanelles and Gallipoli Peninsula. He arrived with the fleet off the Dardanelles in time to observe the Anglo-French fleet's attempt to force the Narrows, and found that Vice Admiral Carden, after a complete nervous breakdown, had been replaced by his deputy, Vice Admiral de Robeck.

The naval attack of the 18th had been defeated, with the loss of three battleships and severe damage to several more. The Germans and Turks had secretly laid an undetected minefield well down the Straits in an area where the bombarding fleet had been manoeuvring, resulting in the spectacular loss of the French pre-dreadnought *Bouvet* with almost her entire crew, together with the elderly British battleships *Ocean* and *Irresistible*. The battlecruiser *Inflexible* and the French battleships *Gaulois* and *Suffren* were severely damaged. The new British super-dreadnought *Queen Elizabeth*, diverted from gunnery trials prior to joining the Grand Fleet, escaped damage, and her eight 15-inch guns wrought considerable destruction on the defences before a furious Fisher ordered her return to home waters, where she joined the Grand Fleet.

It was clear that the fleet would never get through to Marmara unless a large ground force was landed to secure the shores of the Dardanelles and Narrows, where the defenders, although on the verge of collapse at the end of the day on 18 March, had been heartened by success. German advisers supervised the repair of damaged fortifications and the construction of beach defences on the most likely landing places. In command of the Turkish 19th Division

based at Maidos was the unknown Lieutenant Colonel Mustafa Kemal, promoted over the heads of hundreds of others by Liman von Sanders, who had a gift for spotting talent. Kemal trained his command rigorously. Instead of dispersing the defence thinly all around the coast of the peninsula, Liman held the bulk of it well back from the beaches, poised to move rapidly in strength to deal with landings when they came, and holding the main reserve of two divisions back at the Isthmus of Bulair.

The ships bringing equipment out to the Greek islands from England had been loaded

Herbert Asquith, Prime Minister in 1914. He had succeeded to the premiership in 1906 when the health of his Liberal predecessor Campbell-Bannerman broke down. Asquith was immediately faced with diverse problems: Irish Home Rule, the Suffragette movement, and the need to curb the power of the House of Lords, in addition to the oncoming world crisis leading to war. By 1915 he was forced to accept the formation of a war coalition government and was thereafter a victim of the intrigues of his Liberal colleague Lloyd George, who was to succeed him as Prime Minister in 1916. (IWM)

Gallipoli, 1915

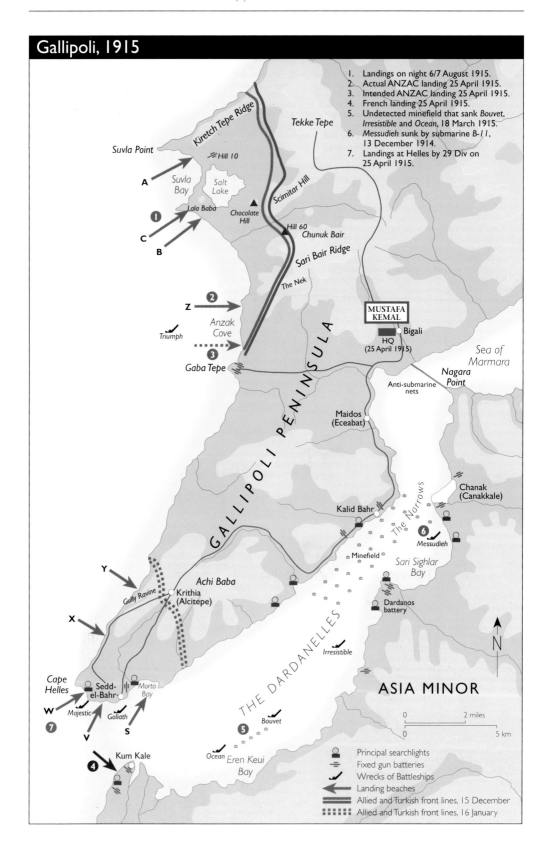

1. Landings on night 6/7 August 1915.
2. Actual ANZAC landing 25 April 1915.
3. Intended ANZAC landing 25 April 1915.
4. French landing 25 April 1915.
5. Undetected minefield that sank *Bouvet*, *Irresistible* and *Ocean*, 18 March 1915.
6. *Messudieh* sunk by submarine *B-11*, 13 December 1914.
7. Landings at Helles by 29 Div on 25 April 1915.

Principal searchlights
Fixed gun batteries
Wrecks of Battleships
Landing beaches
Allied and Turkish front lines, 15 December
Allied and Turkish front lines, 16 January

without thought of what would be needed first after a beach assault. In the absence of wharfage at the harbour of Mudros the ships had to be sent for reloading to Alexandria, where Hamilton established his temporary headquarters. After much haggling in London Kitchener agreed to release the 29th Infantry Division for the eastern Mediterranean. This formation consisted of regular units brought home in the autumn of 1914 from all corners of the empire to join the BEF in France. Over the protests of Field Marshal French and his generals it was shipped to the Mediterranean to join the Anzacs, Royal Naval Division and the French Expeditionary Force commanded by Hamilton's old friend General d'Amade.

Hamilton was told by Admiral de Robeck that the fleet could no longer penetrate deeply into the Dardanelles because of the improved batteries ashore. De Robeck also believed that the Turks had laid further undetected minefields. The plan of attack therefore hinged on landings by the

29th Division under the guns of the fleet at the tip of the peninsula and by the Anzacs some 15 miles up the coast. The Anzac landings were planned to keep Liman's reserve divisions from rushing down to attack the Allied beach-heads. The French were to land at Kum Kale on the Asiatic shore as a further diversion, but would re-embark and join the 29th Division at Helles after two days, Kitchener having specifically forbidden sustained operations on the Asiatic side of the Straits. Given the resources available, Hamilton's plan was imaginative and sound. Its execution was anything but.

The landings took place on the morning of 25 April. The Anzacs went ashore at first light, but were landed a mile north of the

Australian infantry going ashore at Anzac Cove on the morning of 25 April 1915. At this stage the slouch hat had not been universally adopted and most of the troops of the Australian Imperial Force still wore uniforms similar to those of the British army. (IWM)

General Sir Ian Hamilton, Commander-in-Chief at Gallipoli, presents the Military Cross to his French liaison officers at General Headquarters on the island of Imbros. (IWM)

intended beach due to a strong off-shore current. Instead of a gently sloping hinterland and open country all the way to the Narrows (only five miles away across the peninsula) they were confronted with steep slopes – up which they rushed. Their impetus carried them to the heights of the Sari Bair ridge, brushing aside the resistance of Turkish detachments covering the beach; but as they arrived on the summits, blown and disorganised, they met a furious counter-attack led by Mustafa Kemal, which swept them back to the edge of the ridge. There they grimly held on, to positions that became their front line for the rest of the campaign. That night, a despondent Birdwood signalled Hamilton, afloat in the battleship *Queen Elizabeth*, that the situation was so confused that re-embarkation was the only solution. Hamilton ordered him to stick it out and 'Dig, dig, dig', unwittingly creating a legend.

At Helles on the tip of the peninsula the commander of the 29th division, Major General Hunter-Weston, had chosen to land in broad daylight, a decision for which his troops paid dearly. Coming ashore under tow in ship's boats, rowed for the last hundred yards by bluejackets, they came under devastating fire at 'V' beach from the defenders. A naval aviator flying overhead was appalled to see that the water for 50 yards out from the beach was red with

blood. At 'V' beach the landing was augmented by a 'Trojan Horse'. The collier *River Clyde* had been modified, with extra ports in its sides, to beach itself and disgorge two battalions down ramps and across a bridge of boats to the shore. These troops also met withering fire as they emerged from the ship and were pinned down with the others on the shore. At 'W' beach on the other side of Cape Helles, only a mile away, the first battalion ashore, the Lancashire Fusiliers, fought their way off the beach through dense barbed wire, winning six Victoria Crosses in the process. Elsewhere around the Helles area the landings met little resistance, but Hunter-Weston ignored this, concentrating on reinforcing the slaughter at 'W' and 'V'. By last light the 29th Division was shattered and incapable of exploiting inland. The day's final objective, the dominating high ground of Achi Baba, five miles from the landing beaches, was never taken during the campaign.

The French landings at Kum Kale stirred up a hornet's nest and fierce fighting took

The French battleship *Bouvet* rolls over and sinks with almost her entire crew after hitting a mine in the Dardanelles, 18 March 1915. She went down in less than two minutes; as she rolled over her captain turned to his officers on the bridge, ordered them to take to the water and, determined to go down with his ship and crew, locked himself in the conning tower. Less than 40 survivors were picked out of the water. (IWM)

place before the troops were ferried across the straits to join their British comrades at Helles.

Through the furnace heat of summer a series of futile attacks at Helles failed to take Achi Baba or the village of Krithia at its foot. Disease took its toll, brought on by insanitary conditions and the billions of flies feeding on thousands of unburied corpses. The Turkish soldier, previously regarded as no more than an unlettered brute, earned the respect of his opponents. At Anzac, as the precarious beach-head became known, the attackers had to cling to a ridge line subjected to incessant sniper and artillery fire. A great Turkish assault in May, aimed at sweeping the Anzacs into the sea, was fought off, leaving thousands of putrefying dead in the open. So appalling was

Lt Commander Holbrook and the crew of the submarine *B-11* following the successful attack that sank the ancient Turkish battleship *Messudieh* off Chanak, gaining Holbrook the VC, his second-in-command the DSO, and the entire crew the DSM. Convinced that they would not return from this hazardous mission, officers and crew had written last letters home; before carrying out the attack all ate a good meal in their cramped quarters on *B-11*; the two officers shared a large lobster and the ratings devoured a York Ham. (IWM)

the smell and health hazard that a truce was agreed in which both sides buried their dead, fraternising briefly as they did so.

Hamilton's force was now effectively stranded and Kitchener belatedly sent reinforcements: a territorial division from Egypt, and another from Scotland. Both were committed to ill-planned and costly attacks producing little or no gain. More troops were called for: territorial divisions stripped of their best officers and men to feed the Western Front, and partly-trained 'Kitchener' divisions shipped out to the eastern Mediterranean as the 9th Army Corps, for what Hamilton hoped would be the decisive battle. His August offensive aimed to take

the summits of the Sari Bair ridge; a diversionary attack at Helles was to pin down Turkish reinforcements, and the 9th Corps made a new landing some miles north of Anzac, in Suvla Bay. In theory a sound plan, it was disastrously bungled by the commanders on the ground, while Hamilton fumed impotently at his headquarters on the island of Imbros. Lieutenant General Sir Frederick Stopford, commanding 9th Corps, had been picked out of retirement, as had many of his subordinates. The citizen soldiers landed at Suvla were virtually all volunteers; patriotic, brave, bewildered and worthy of far better leadership than they got.

The assault on the Sari Bair Heights was pressed home with utmost courage by New Zealanders who drove the Turks off Chunuk Bair. A diversionary attack by the Australian Light Horse serving as infantry along a ridge line known as The Nek (graphically portrayed in the film *Gallipoli*) failed despite the Australians' sublime gallantry. Elsewhere on Sari Bair a battalion of Gurkhas reached the summit, only to be destroyed by 'friendly fire'. At Helles the diversionary assault also failed. Mustafa Kemal, in command of the defence at Sari Bair, ordered a massive counter-attack on 10 August that swept all before it as the close-packed Turkish infantry surged over the crest. The objective of the last great British attack, on 21st August, included a spur known as Scimitar Hill. The attack failed amidst scenes of horror as the scrub ignited, cremating hundreds of wounded in the blazing undergrowth.

No further offensive action was possible at Gallipoli; priority for reinforcements went to the Western Front, and the need to send troops to Salonika progressively weakened the force's ability to do any more than hold on. Hamilton was recalled in October and replaced by General Monro, who took stock of the dismal situation and immediately recommended evacuation, prompting an embittered Churchill (shifted from the Admiralty to the anodyne appointment of Chancellor of the Duchy

of Lancaster) to comment: 'He came, he saw, he capitulated'.

The naval campaign in the Dardanelles had started with the exploit of submarine B-11 followed by the leisurely bombardment of the forts and the disastrous attempt to force the Narrows on 18 March. It took a turn for the worse in mid-May with the loss of the battleship *Goliath*, and the arrival in the eastern Mediterranean of a number of U-boats. Two more pre-dreadnoughts, *Triumph* and *Majestic*, were torpedoed in full view of the horrified troops ashore, and most

King George V reviewing the 29th Division at Dunchurch, near Coventry, prior to embarkation for Gallipoli. This was to be the last time a regular division of the 'old army' would parade for their monarch. Eyewitnesses testify to the magnificent spectacle as the battalions marched past, ranked in double fours, to the music of the massed bands. Guns, horses and men were superbly turned out and the king, visibly excited galloped with his entourage down the ranks to watch this historic parade as it dispersed. (IWM)

An extraordinary picture, taken by a machine gunner in the bows of the *River Clyde* during the landing at 'V' Beach, Helles, on the morning of 25 April 1915. The converted collier was fitted with ports in its sides through which the infantry onboard could descend along inclined ramps and go ashore along a bridge of lighters. Sandbagged machine gun positions were built on the bows, manned by the Royal Naval Air Service. Men of the Royal Munster Fusiliers ashore can be seen taking cover under the walls of Sedd-el-Bahr castle; many others lay dead, piled on the decks of the lighters. So great was the slaughter to the Munsters that the disembarkation of the Hampshires was cancelled until after dark. (IWM)

of the fleet abruptly departed to safer anchorages in the Greek islands, a move that further lowered the morale of the army ashore. As the U-boats ran riot, sinking numerous troopships with great loss of life, the situation at sea got worse. In one aspect, however, the navy earned undying fame. Ever since the initial landings, boldly handled British Australian and French submarines had braved the Dardanelles defences to force their way into the Sea of Marmara to eliminate the Turkish merchant marine. They sank numerous warships and on several occasions penetrated into the harbour at Constantinople, causing widespread panic. Naval aviation also played a prominent part. Kitchener had expressly prohibited the use of the Royal Flying Corps in the expeditionary force but the Royal Naval Air Service, initially equipped with underpowered primitive machines, grew in strength and confidence to the extent that it scored the first success with torpedo-carrying floatplanes against Turkish ships in the Sea of Marmara.

The approach of winter brought torrential rain, followed by hard frost and snow, creating appalling conditions for the hapless infantry in their open trenches. Thousands were evacuated with frostbite, hypothermia and trench foot; hundreds froze to death. Kitchener briefly came to see things for himself and, aghast at what he had required of Hamilton and his troops, confirmed the order for evacuation. On the nights of 19 December 1915 and 8 January 1916 the troops at Anzac-Suvla, then Helles, were taken off from under the noses of the unsuspecting Turks in a brilliantly planned and executed operation in which not a single man was lost.

Of some 410,000 British and Empire troops and 70,000 French who went ashore, 252,000 were killed, wounded, missing, prisoners or evacuated sick. Estimates of Turkish casualties vary between 218,000 and 400,000 with at least 66,000 killed in action. Great heroism was displayed on both sides but to pit inexperienced troops against the best of the Turkish army, fighting for its own soil and fired by patriotism, was asking too

The superdreadnought HMS *Queen Elizabeth* leaving Mudros harbour to bombard the Dardanelles forts with her eight 15-inch guns. Traces of the damage caused by these guns are still to be seen at Canakkale (Chanak) where the 15th-century Cimenlik castle was hit several times. Note the painted false bow wave, to deceive the range-takers of the shore batteries. (IWM)

much. Amphibious operations are the hardest of all to bring off, requiring careful training and rehearsal, neither of which were given the soldiers that fought at Gallipoli.

Defence of the Suez Canal

Egypt, technically still part of the Ottoman Empire in 1914, had been under effective control of a British 'Agent' since 1882. The army was in the hands of a British Commander-in-Chief or *Sirdar*. British officials headed most government departments in Egypt including the police. The nominal Egyptian head of government and viceroy of the Ottoman Sultan was the *Khedive*, Abbas El Hilmi: an anglophobe mostly resident in Constantinople, he was summarily deposed by the British in

December 1914. The British closure of the Canal in August 1914 to ships of hostile nations was illegal under international law but reasonable in the circumstances. The small British peacetime garrison of regular troops was replaced by territorial infantry and mounted Yeomanry, joined before Christmas by the vanguard of the Australians and New Zealanders destined for the Western Front.

The declaration of *jihad* or holy war by the Sultan in his capacity as Caliph in November was ignored where it should most have taken fire – the holy places of Islam in Arabia. Sherif Hussein of Mecca and his extended Hashemite family saw that the grip of the Sultan had slipped to the extent that they could make a bid for power on their own account. But there were places where the idea of holy war did appeal to Muslim leaders. The Libyan provinces of Tripolitania and Cyrenaica, under Italian control since 1912, were inhabited by tribes owing religious and some political loyalty to Ahmad al-Sharif, Grand Senussi of Sollum. Known collectively as the Senussi these people had fought against the Italians with the help of Turkish advisers. In 1914 the Turks sought Senussi aid in distracting British attention from the Suez Canal, and in the hope of spreading *jihad* westwards to afflict the French in their North African territories.

West of the Nile delta rises a low plateau; to the south extends the great Libyan desert, its boundary marked by a string of great oases whose inhabitants acknowledged the authority of Senussi Ahmad. Nominally a dependant of the Egyptian government, he was required to keep the tribes in reasonable order. The Turks saw an opportunity to re-assert their authority in this area early in 1915 when Enver sent his half brother Nuri Bey to the Senussi, accompanied by one Jafar Pasha, a German officer who had embraced Islam. If Ahmad proclaimed his own holy war against the British in Egypt, he was promised German money and arms. Intelligence of Nuri's and Jafar's activities reached GHQ in Cairo and measures were taken to forestall insurrection spreading into Egypt, where many of the Delta peasantry owed allegiance to Senussi Ahmad as their religious leader. An improvised Western Desert Force assembled at Alexandria including British, Australians, New Zealanders, South Africans, Sikhs of the Indian Army, and Egyptians. Apart from skirmishes along the frontier, little happened until the end of 1915, by which time the Senussi had received several shipments of German arms. Some sharp encounters took place on ground destined to become familiar in the Second World War.

In January 1916 the Grand Senussi, emerging from his base in the great Siwa oasis, personally led an advance eastward along the coast from Mersah Matruh with a force commanded by Jafar. In what turned out to be the decisive engagement of this miniature campaign, at Aqqaquia on 26 February, the Western Desert Force defeated and captured Jafar, who, having recovered from his wounds, changed sides to become a successful commander of one of Sherif Hussein's irregular armies in the Arab Revolt.

Turkish and German eyes turned toward the Canal as the vital focus of a strategy threatening Egypt, the coaling and signal station at Aden, British interests in the Persian Gulf, and India. The Turks needed little persuasion to mount a major operation against the Canal, assigning it to their 8th Army under Djemal Pasha, whose Chief of Staff, Colonel (later General) Baron Friedrich Kress von Kressenstein boldly decided early in 1915 to approach the canal by a direct march across the Sinai desert. Water was the great problem. The force had to cover about 120 miles from Gaza in Palestine to Kantara on the Canal; at least 12 days supply was needed for men, horses and camels. A diversionary force advanced down the Mediterranean coast, while the main body advanced across Sinai to halt in an area close to the canal where a tract of sand dunes offered cover as pontoons and collapsible boats carried across the desert were assembled. To manhandle these and field artillery across Sinai was a remarkable feat. The defenders, alerted by aerial reconnaissance, deployed to meet the threat. During the night of 1 February several attempts were made to get across the Canal but few Turks made it. At dawn next day the battle spread as further Turkish units reached the Canal. Gunboats hastened to the scene and shot the Turkish boats out of the water. The Turks withdrew, taking their guns with them back over the Sinai. There was no further action on the canal in 1915, and General Maxwell strengthened the defences. At one time that year he commanded no less than 13 divisions but these were progressively withdrawn to meet crises elsewhere in the theatre.

Advance into Sinai and Palestine

Early in 1916 Lieutenant General Sir Archibald Murray succeeded Maxwell; his command was re-designated the Egyptian Expeditionary Force, including all troops in the Eastern Mediterranean theatre. Murray was ordered to begin a deliberate advance up the coast towards Palestine. The cavalry patrolled deep into the desert on his landward flank. A railway and a water

War in the desert, 1915–18

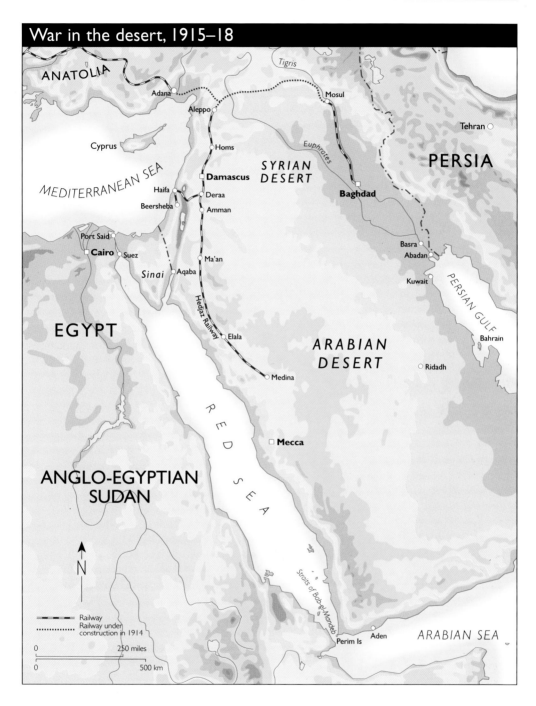

pipeline accompanied the laborious advance as the rough track was improved to take heavy motor transport. Kress harassed the advance effectively, but by the end of May 1916 Murray had set up a railhead at El Rumana, deploying a division to defend it. Realising that Kress would try to turn his right flank, Murray threw out a force of cavalry; the Turks attacked this vigorously on 4 August and were beaten off, suffering heavily in the process. The Turkish soldier was already recognised as a formidable opponent, brave and enduring; respect for him mounted accordingly.

By the end of 1916 the British had edged forward against stubborn resistance to El Arish, less than 30 miles from the border of Palestine. The vigour of the Turks defending the frontier posts at Maghdaba and Rafah warned Murray to advance cautiously, the first major objective being the town of Gaza. Murray placed Major General Sir Charles Dobell in charge of the operation. Dobell had masses of mounted troops, including General Chetwode's 'Desert Column' but they brought with them the problem of watering 10,000 horses. The wells at Gaza were therefore essential to success. The town, protected by a natural barrier of dense cactus hedges, was held by 4,000 determined Turks. Dobell decided to shield his right flank with

Austrian machine gun crew in action in the snow. The weapon is the standard Austrian issue Schwarzlose M 7/12. A company of these guns formed part of the establishment of the infantry regiment. The Schwarzlose had a rate of fire of 450–500 rounds a minute, using the standard M-95 rifle ammunition in belts of 250 rounds. It was mounted on a tripod which could incorporate a metal protective shield for the crew; the total weight came to 170 lbs. (IWM)

cavalry and attack frontally from the south. On 26 March 1917 the infantry advanced in a dense fog and all went well until the cavalry, short of water, had to be recalled. Due to a staff error the infantry also retired from positions they had gained, which had to be retaken next day. Kress counter-attacked and drove in Dobell's right flank. At this point the battle was broken off.

The second battle of Gaza took place on 17 April. By now the Turks had improved their positions and were strongly dug in along the line of the Gaza-Beersheba road. Dobell decided to attack on a two-mile frontage with a single division. Although he had given Dobell *carte blanche* in the execution of the attack, Murray entirely neglected to check the staff-work, resulting in hopeless muddle and failure. The attackers sustained 6,500 casualties to 2,000 Turkish losses. Murray was held to blame by London and removed from command in June. His relief, from the 3rd Army in France, was General Sir Edmund Allenby, who insisted on getting all the reinforcements he asked

Review of Turkish, Austrian and German troops in Palestine by Djemal Pasha. Although a reasonably competent commander his German allies lost confidence in him and he was side-tracked after the battles of Gaza and replaced by German generals. (IWM)

for and visited every unit in his command to restore morale. A large man (known as 'The Bull') with a terrible temper, his evident professionalism quickly motivated the troops and gained their unqualified support.

Allenby's force was substantially reinforced. Two mounted divisions were formed in Egypt and two more came from Mesopotamia and Macedonia. He now had seven infantry divisions, and formed them into two army corps, under Generals Chetwode and Bulfin. After careful personal reconnaissance he planned two hammer blows, at Gaza and Beersheba. The Turks would be pinned down at the former as the Anzacs took Beersheba and its essential water supplies. Some tanks (the only ones to leave the Western Front in the entire war) had been sent to Palestine and made their debut at Beersheba, which was taken on

21 October. The Turks failed to destroy the vital wells and their whole line was rolled up from east to west; Gaza was bombarded by the Anglo-French fleet and occupied on 16 November. This battle, known as '3rd Gaza' was the start of a victorious progress for Allenby and his rejuvenated army.

The Germans, alarmed by the turn of events, sent one of their star performers, General Erich von Falkenhayn, to sort things out. Having rejected a hare-brained scheme of Enver's to retake Baghdad, he launched an attack on Allenby's vulnerable right flank but lacked resources for a decisive result. After much bitter fighting, Jerusalem fell and Allenby entered the city on foot on 11 December. The symbolic humility of the gesture was not lost on the world at large.

Torrential rains now halted the campaign. In March 1918 Allenby pushed east to Amman in Transjordan to cut the Hedjaz railway that supplied all the Turkish garrisons to the south. The foray was unsuccessful; although Amman was besieged, the primary target, a great railway viaduct,

Campaigns in Sinai and Palestine, 1914–18

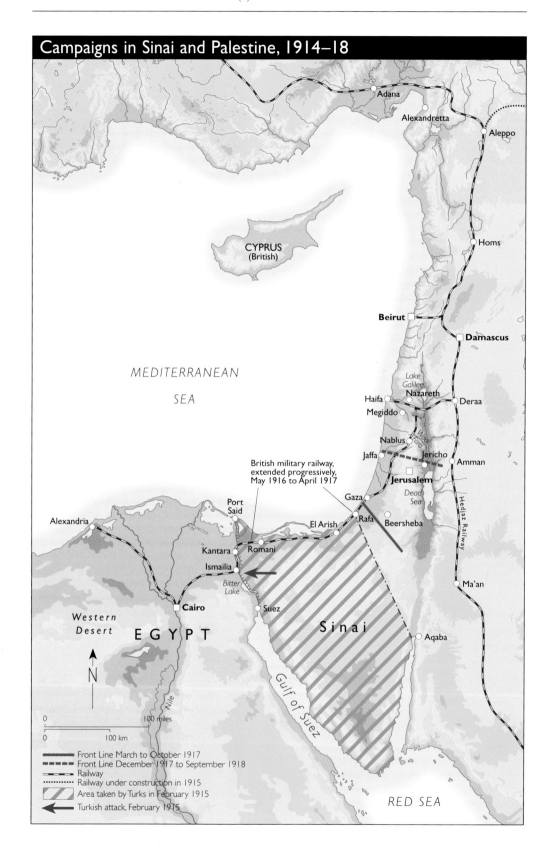

Adana

Alexandretta

Aleppo

Homs

CYPRUS
(British)

Beirut

Damascus

MEDITERRANEAN

SEA

Lake
Galilee

Haifa   Nazareth   Deraa

Megiddo

Nablus

Jaffa   Jericho   Amman

Jerusalem

Dead
Sea

British military railway,
extended progressively,
May 1916 to April 1917

Gaza

Port
Said

El Arish   Rafa   Beersheba

Alexandria

Kantara   Romani

Ismailia

Bitter
Lake

Cairo   Suez

Western
Desert   EGYPT

Sinai   Aqaba

Hedjaz Railway

Ma'an

N

Nile

Gulf of Suez

0   100 miles
0   100 km

Front Line March to October 1917
Front Line December 1917 to September 1918
Railway
Railway under construction in 1915
Area taken by Turks in February 1915
Turkish attack, February 1915

RED SEA

Megiddo, Allenby's master stroke, 16–20 September 1918

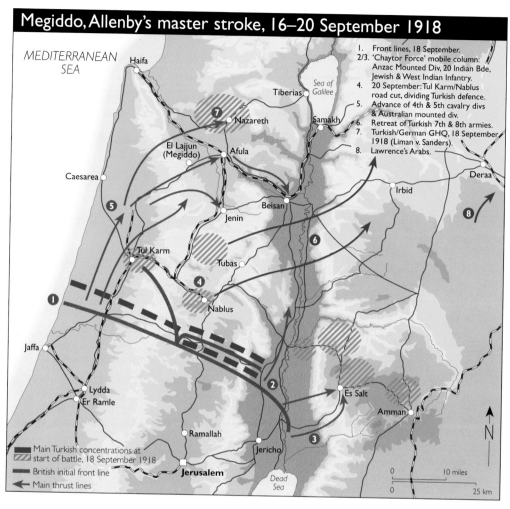

MEDITERRANEAN SEA

1. Front lines, 18 September.
2/3. 'Chaytor Force' mobile column: Anzac Mounted Div, 20 Indian Bde, Jewish & West Indian Infantry.
4. 20 September: Tul Karm/Nablus road cut, dividing Turkish defence.
5. Advance of 4th & 5th cavalry divs & Australian mounted div.
6. Retreat of Turkish 7th & 8th armies.
7. Turkish/German GHQ, 18 September 1918 (Liman v. Sanders).
8. Lawrence's Arabs.

Haifa, Tiberias, Sea of Galilee, Samakh, Nazareth, El Lajjun (Megiddo), Afula, Caesarea, Deraa, Irbid, Beisan, Jenin, Tul Karm, Tubas, Nablus, Jaffa, Lydda, Er Ramle, Ramallah, Jericho, Jerusalem, Es Salt, Amman, Dead Sea

Main Turkish concentrations at start of battle, 18 September 1918
British initial front line
Main thrust lines

0   10 miles
0   25 km

N

remained intact. The German March offensive in France deprived Allenby of many of his best units – a total of 90,000 men in two infantry divisions, nine Yeomanry regiments and some of the heavy artillery went to France. Allenby's force now included untried Indian Army troops but also a splendid Indian cavalry division that had been wasted in France. He still enjoyed a two-to-one numerical superiority over the Turks, whose strength had never exceeded 30,000, but there was still one German division in Palestine, well trained and heavily armed.

In Arabia, stirrings of nationalism were already evident and Sherif Hussein, to whom Kitchener had already offered conditional independence, began negotiations with the

Allenby, who had studied his military history, followed a plan used by a victorious Egyptian army around 1480 BC. Covering his right flank with a small mobile force pushing up the Jordan valley under General Chaytor as Lawrence's Arabs cut the railway north of Deraa, he pinned the Turkish left as his cavalry drove through on the coast, then turned inland. The Turks, threatened with envelopment, retreated north east in disorder; Otto Liman von Sanders only narrowly escaped capture as his GHQ was over-run.

British in 1915. Hussein's terms were explicit; he would fight the Turks in return for recognition of independence for Arab countries south of the 37th parallel of latitude; this was rejected by the British as it would have included large tracts of Asia Minor and Syria. A compromise was reached, although the future of Baghdad and Basra was left vague.

As Hussein had to be armed and financed it was not until mid-1916 that the Arab revolt got under way in the Hedjaz with an attack on the Turkish garrison of Medina. Hussein proclaimed the independence of the Hedjaz and the garrison of Mecca surrendered in June. Hussein then, to the consternation of the British government, proclaimed himself King of all the Arabs and appealed to Arabs everywhere to take up arms against the Turks. His claim of kingship of the Hedjaz was recognised by London at the end of the year.

The course of the Arab revolt was punctuated by quarrels between various factions and tribes involved, and the duplicity of British and French politicians preparing their respective post-war spheres of influence in the Near East. The key British personality on the ground was the gifted Captain (later Colonel) T E Lawrence, a young Oxford archaeologist with profound knowledge of, and sympathy for, the Arab cause. Working for the Arab Bureau, he gained the confidence of Hussein and his sons and quickly revealed a genius for guerrilla warfare, leading highly mobile columns of camel-mounted irregulars to attack the vulnerable Hedjaz railway, cutting the tracks, blowing bridges along its length and overwhelming isolated garrisons. By mid-1917 Lawrence and his men were ranging widely and on 3 June, while sounding out the Syrian Arab tribes, they blew up a length of the Aleppo-Damascus railway. A month later Lawrence took the surrender of the Turkish garrison at Aqaba, then went to Cairo to meet Allenby and discuss future operations. Allenby recognised Lawrence's talents and agreed to co-operate. By the end of the year the two men were co-ordinating operations with the Arab irregulars to inflict maximum disruption on the Turks and their German Allies. Having disposed of the Hedjaz railway, for which the stocks of replacement rails had long run out, Lawrence protected Allenby's right flank in the offensive both hoped would end the campaign. The Turks were now commanded by the talented Otto Liman von Sanders who had a small German contingent and three

shaky Turkish armies at his disposal. On 19 September 1918 Allenby struck. His plan for the attack at Megiddo relied on secrecy, deception and surprise. The Turkish right flank collapsed, and Liman only narrowly avoided capture when his command post was overrun. On 20 September the British crossed the Jordan as Nazareth fell and Allenby's cavalry were loosed in pursuit. The Turkish armies collapsed and the 7th, caught as it jammed the Wadi Fara, was virtually destroyed in a lethal bombing attack by aircraft of the RAF. Allenby and Lawrence entered Damascus simultaneously on 1 October, Beirut fell to the French on 7 October and by the end of the month they had occupied Homs and Aleppo.

This was the end for the Ottoman armies. The new Turkish Sultan, Mehmet VI, sacked the Young Turk ministry and appealed to President Wilson of the United States to seek an armistice on Turkey's behalf. In the absence of a reply the Turks took the bizarre step of releasing General Townshend from his comfortable detention, sending him as their emissary to Admiral Calthorpe, Flag Officer Royal Navy in the Aegean. The armistice was signed at Mudros on the island of Lemnos on 30 October. Under its terms Turkey opened the Dardanelles, released all prisoners of war, formally ended her alliance with the Central Powers, and placed Turkish territory at the Allies' disposal for further operations of war. On 12 November the Allied fleet passed through the Chanak Narrows and sailed to Constantinople, where the great city lay under its guns.

The Italian campaign

At the end of 1914 Italy was being courted by both the Central Powers and the Allies. The Italian government had prudently declared neutrality on 3 August, despite the implications of the Triple Alliance that should have taken Italy into the war on the side of Germany and Austria. Her army and navy were the most powerful of the neutrals in Europe and her geographical position was strategically important, lying on the flanks of both the Central Powers and the Allies. Italy had the naval power to control the Mediterranean sea lanes, notably in the Sicilian Narrows, where a combined Austro-Italian navy could have denied access to the Suez Canal. But intensive diplomatic and political activity secured Italy's signature to the Treaty of London in April 1915, bringing her into alliance with Great Britain, France, Belgium and Russia for prosecution of war against Austria, against whom Italy declared war on 24 May.

The Austro-Italian frontier had been created artificially by a Treaty in 1866 engineered by Bismarck, providing Austria with a barrier of mountains from which her army could sweep down at will onto the north Italian Plain. Any Italian offensive would have to be conducted uphill. Italy's difficulties were increased by the shape of the frontier, a giant 'S' on its side, with a huge salient projecting into Italy in the Trentino district, and the Udine salient extending into Austrian territory. Of these the Trentino was potentially the more dangerous, but its poor road and rail

communications also presented problems to Austria's military planners. From the Swiss border to the Adriatic the battle line extended for nearly 400 miles, divided into three segments: Trentino, Alpine, and Isonzo. Except for about 30 moderately hilly miles on the Isonzo, the entire line lay in mountain terrain. Anticipating war with Austria, whose intentions towards her former Venetian provinces were all too clear, Italy had fortified all three fronts, covering the

June 1915. Field Marshal Lord Kitchener reviews troops of the 10th (Irish) division prior to their embarkation for the eastern Mediterranean. This formation, commanded by Lieutenant General Sir Bryan Mahon, had been initially raised and trained by him in Ireland as a 'New Army' division, but as the response of the southern Irish to Kitchener's appeal for volunteers was predictably luke-warm its battalions had been substantially fleshed out with surplus volunteers from over-recruited Yorkshire and Lancashire regiments. Eyewitnesses of this parade, held near Basingstoke, long remembered the sight of 'K' mounted on a huge black charger, 'immobile as a graven image' as the battalions trooped past him. If he entertained doubts as to the prudence of dispatching such raw units to fight the Turks, his impassive features revealed nothing. (IWM)

Lord Kitchener reviewing the 10th Division at Basingstoke. June 1-15.

northern Plain with a network of strategic roads and railways to permit rapid movement of troops to any threatened sector. On their side of the frontier the Austrian General Staff had constructed permanent defensive positions and had improved the transportation infrastructure in the rear areas. The existence of fixed defences on both sides dictated that from the outset the campaign would be mainly static.

The Italian Chief of Staff General Cadorna planned to attack on the Isonzo front, where the objectives of Trieste and the route to Vienna lay within reach, along with the tempting opportunity to link with the armies of Serbia and Russia. The Italians' Achilles heel was the Trentino front, where a successful Austrian breakthrough would isolate Cadorna's armies on the Isonzo. The lay-out of the Italian railway system in the region acknowledged this; a double-track route ran parallel to the frontier, with spurs branching off up the valleys. The Austrian rail system provided a main line following their side of the frontier but was deficient in branch lines, and this was eventually to lose them the momentum of their offensive in Trentino.

On the outbreak of hostilities the Italians deployed 35 divisions, facing some 20 Austrian divisions in strong, near-impregnable positions along the front. Soldiers of both sides faced arduous conditions in the mountains. Cadorna planned a sustained offensive on the Isonzo and aggressive defence on the Trentino, whilst securing advantageous positions for his *Alpini* fighting in the high Carnic Alps. The Italian army was ill-prepared, having exhausted most of its material reserves in the Libyan war, and left-wing political pressure had prevented their replacement. Artillery, machine guns, and the materials for constructing field defences were all deficient. The air wing, eventually to become outstandingly effective, was still at an early stage of development.

Despite these problems the Italians advanced on all fronts on 23 May 1915, surprising the Austrians. Initial results were gratifying and the Italians secured a number

of positions inside Austrian territory on the Isonzo front, where the line stabilised, setting the scene for successive attritional battles. The first of these got under way on 23 June – 11 more would almost bleed the Italian army white. At the same time, however, these bloody slogging matches, resembling the Allied offensives in France, were also to drain the Austrian war effort and pin down whole armies badly needed on the Eastern Front.

General Count Luigi Cadorna came from an old Piedmontese military family. His father had commanded the army that entered Rome in 1870, sealing Italian unity. On the death of General Pollo in 1914 Cadorna saw that the army was operationally unfit, and did much in the next few months to prepare it for war. From the outbreak of war he persisted with repeated head-on assaults, incurring enormous casualties. An austere and aloof man, ruthless to under-performing subordinates, he lacked the humanity that endears successful generals to their men. By the end of 1915 he had fought four battles on the Isonzo, struggling to take the important town of Gorizia, protected by an Austrian bridgehead and covered by fire from surrounding hills. The Austrian positions were enormously strong and both sides suffered terrible casualties. These were titanic battles; in the 2nd battle of the Isonzo the Italians pitched 260 battalions against 129 Austrian, but despite this superiority the defences proved too strong. Cadorna, never noted for his tolerance, had already sacked 27 generals and he removed many more in the months ahead. In their first four Isonzo attacks alone the Italians lost 161,000 men and the Austrians nearly 147,000 killed, wounded, captured and missing. More Italians were called from the reserve to the colours. One 32-year-old reservist rejoining the *Bersaglieri* in August 1915 was destined to make his mark on Italian history – Benito Mussolini, the editor of a socialist newspaper, was invalided out of the army following injuries sustained in a trench mortar accident, but not before he had been decorated for gallantry.

The Italian front, 1915–18

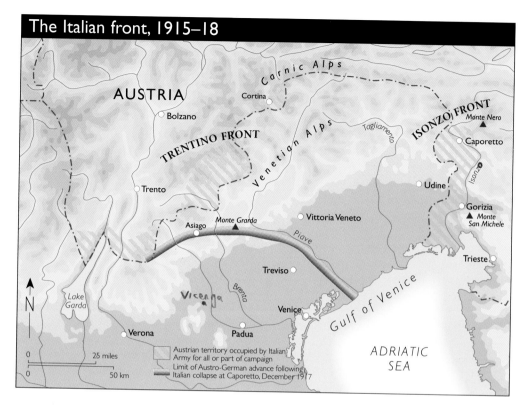

As winter descended the tempo of operations slowed, and cholera, supposedly contracted from the Austrians, spread through the Italian army. The Italians were still short of artillery, especially the heavy guns needed to break up the Austrian defences. At an Allied summit conference at Chantilly it was agreed that Britain and France would provide additional guns and equipment to buttress the Italian war effort.

The Austrian Chief of Staff, Conrad, was expected by his German Allies to concentrate his main efforts against the Russians, freeing German formations for use on the Western Front. But he had ideas of his own. One was to mount a decisive attack in the Trentino, advancing rapidly across the Italian Plain to seize the great cities of the north. He selected the area around the Asiago plateau for the attack. The prospect appalled the Chief of the German General Staff, General Erich von Falkenhayn. Conrad held on to a mass of heavy artillery that Falkenhayn badly needed to reduce the French forts at Verdun, and his Trentino plan diverted a number of divisions

from the Eastern Front. Falkenhayn also believed that the 18 divisions assembled by Conrad would prove inadequate, even though the Austrians enjoyed a marked superiority in artillery – 2,000 guns including nearly 500 pieces of heavy artillery against the Italians' 588 field and 36 heavy guns.

The Trentino attack began at dawn on 15 May 1916, using the novelty of a short but concentrated artillery bombardment that virtually destroyed the Italian trench systems. The Austrian heavy artillery was devastating in the confined valleys, causing avalanches and rock falls; but the rugged terrain saved the Italians from overwhelming defeat, as it slowed the Austrian advance to a crawl. The skill of the *Alpini*, fighting on their home ground, bought time for the defence to stabilise. Even so, by 4 June the Austrians, who had captured the Italian code books and were intercepting their wireless traffic, were within 20 miles of Vicenza and the vital lateral railway supplying the Isonzo front. Here they ran out of momentum, and Cadorna's counter-attack on 16 June steadily drove the Austrians back to their start lines. Falkenhayn was furious, for by diverting troops and guns from the east, Conrad had enabled the Russian General Brusilov to launch a successful offensive.

Five further battles of the Isonzo took place in 1916 as casualties mounted. The Italians were rewarded in August by the capture of Gorizia and briefly it seemed that a breakthrough had been achieved; but the momentum went out of the attack. Cadorna had done better than he had hoped, with gains of up to four miles on a 15-mile front. With the return of winter, offensive action once more came to a virtual halt apart from raids and patrols.

At an Allied conference in Rome in January 1917, Cadorna called for eight British and French divisions and 300 heavy guns to capture Trieste and knock Austria out of the war. He was promised artillery, but only on loan for two or three months. The situation in Macedonia, where pressure on Salonika was increasing, made equally urgent demands on the Allies, and the Russian Revolution, beginning in March, enabled the Austrians to transfer formations from the east to augment their forces on the Isonzo and Trentino fronts. Undeterred, Cadorna ordered two further attacks, the 10th and 11th, on the Isonzo. At the end of August the Italians seemed on the point of final victory; Austrian morale was crumbling as non-Germanic regiments lost their stomach for the war. The Allies had responded to Cadorna's pleas for heavy artillery and British 6-inch batteries were serving under his command. General Ludendorff, Falkenhayn's successor as Chief of Staff, recognised that Austrian political and military collapse could follow a 12th battle of the Isonzo and sent massive reinforcements for Conrad's army. These included elite German units trained in new tactics whereby assault troops ('storm troops'), advancing rapidly, by-passed centres of resistance and struck at the enemy's headquarters and gun lines. In one such unit served an officer with a future. Major Erwin Rommel commanded a company in a

Württemberg mountain battalion that was to play a key role in the forthcoming 12th battle of the Isonzo.

In this battle the newly formed 14th Austro-German army came close to winning the campaign outright. Its commander was General Otto von Below, who had an outstanding record of victories already to his credit. Italian military intelligence had correctly predicted the date and place of the offensive. The Italian line was held at the point of attack by the 2nd Army, whose commander, General Capello, a sick man, relinquished command on 20 October. His dispositions were better suited to the offensive than a sound defence (an Italian offensive had been planned, but postponed), as became clear when von Below attacked near Caporetto early on the 24th. A storm of artillery overwhelmed the 2nd Army, destroying its fieldworks and throwing its communications into chaos. Gas was widely used and the Italian respirators proved ineffective. Fog and rain helped the storm troops to infiltrate the Italian rear areas. The 14th Army crossed the Isonzo and by nightfall on the first day von Below had penetrated the Italian reserve lines and taken the high ground on the defenders' side of the river. The 2nd Army disintegrated, although some units stood firm as the German storm troops swept round them. So great was the impetus of the attack that a withdrawal to an intermediate line ordered by Capello, who rose from his sick bed only to collapse again, was overtaken by the onrushing Germans. On the left of the 2nd Army, the 3rd army commanded by the Duke of Aosta held firm, but as its flank was about to be turned, it was ordered to conform with the flight of the hapless 2nd. There was huge congestion on the roads to the rear. Bridges were blown by panicky engineers before retreating units had reached them. Across the plains immense crowds of men and animals poured back towards the Tagliamento river where Cadorna intended to stand. Thousands of men from the 2nd Army were demobilising themselves, discarding arms, uniforms and equipment as they sought by any means to get away from the battle area and make their way home (a situation graphically depicted in Ernest Hemingway's *A Farewell to Arms*). The 3rd Army, however, retained its discipline and cohesion.

Senior French and British generals visited the front to assess the damage as soldiers of both nations arrived in Italy to buttress the line. Sir William Robertson, Chief of the Imperial General Staff, advised Cadorna to fight on and hold the river lines. Foch, never one to mince his words, told Cadorna that he '... had only lost one army!' and should fight on with the rest. The retreat went on and the Tagliamento Line was abandoned. The last-ditch stand had to be made on the line of the Piave, where the defenders dug in on 7 November. They were barely 20 miles from Venice as Cadorna issued his last Order of the Day, predictably exhorting his troops '... to die and not to yield' before he was replaced by General Armando Diaz, an equally capable but far more humane soldier. The line held and Diaz took stock. 12th Isonzo, or Caporetto as it became known, had been a catastrophe. The Italians lost 10,000 killed, 30,000 wounded, a staggering 265,000 taken prisoner, and untold thousands of deserters. Losses of equipment were equally calamitous: over 3,000 guns, 3,000 machine guns, almost 2,000 mortars, and vast quantities of stores and equipment.

This disaster had several surprising results. The Allies at last decided that a unified command was needed if Germany was to be brought low. An emergency summit held at Versailles created a Supreme War Council, leading at last to unified operational policies. Simultaneously, an astonishing spirit of national unity blazed in Italy; thanks to inspirational public speaking and writing by an oddly-assorted pair, the poet and aviator Gabriele d'Annunzio and the socialist journalist Mussolini. A surge of patriotism drove hundreds of thousands to enlist and make good the losses at Caporetto. Prime Minister Orlando told his deputies that Italy

would never surrender even if the army had to be withdrawn to Sicily. Diaz went quietly about the task of restoring his army, reinforced by French and British troops, guns and aircraft sent hurriedly from the Western Front. Morale rose again as the enemy, exhausted by their efforts and short of food, gave up trying to pierce the Allied line.

1917 had been a bad year for the Allies. The French army had mutinied and the Russian revolution continued to spread, freeing some of the Central Powers' armies for action elsewhere. But America had at last entered the war and the Germans knew that her vast resources would decide the outcome if Germany could not achieve the decisive breakthrough soon.

Throughout the spring and summer of 1918, as matters hung in the balance in France, the Italian front was quiet; Diaz, determined to give his army time to recover from Caporetto, declined to attack until ordered to do so by Premier Orlando in October. By now the Italians had been augmented by significant French and British forces. Orlando believed an attack now was essential in order to gain bargaining power at the conference table – all the signs indicated that the Austro-Hungarian empire was about to collapse. The offensive launched by Diaz on 24 October proved Orlando correct. As the Allied army attacked at Vittorio Veneto the Austrians broke and ran. A rout ensued, with mutiny and mass desertions by Serbian, Croatian, Czech and Polish troops. Mutiny also broke out in the Austrian navy and on 3 November Austria signed armistice terms. The war in Italy was over.

Salonika and Macedonia

As the last Serbian troops were evacuated from Albania by sea in January 1916 the Allies realised they had missed a golden opportunity in failing to insist that the Greeks honoured their treaty obligation to go to Serbia's aid in the event of a Bulgarian invasion. The Serbs had outfought the Austrians, but the Bulgarian invasion proved

Russian troops arriving at Salonika before marching along the waterfront to music of a British army band. Until the effects of the Russian revolution began to sap their morale and discipline, these troops fought well as part of the Allied command. (IWM)

too much. A combined Serbian and Greek army would have deterred Bulgarian ambitions and blocked passage from Germany to Constantinople over the Berlin-Baghdad railway.

French and British troops began to arrive at Salonika in the late summer of 1915, initially from Gallipoli where stalemate had set in after Hamilton's ill-starred August offensive. From October to December several abortive attempts were made to link up with the Serbs but the Bulgars drove the French back over the Greek border. At a conference held at Chantilly in December it was agreed that a Franco-British force would hold Salonika despite the defeat of Serbia. Meanwhile King Constantine of the Hellenes pledged his friendship for the Allies but declined to join them against the Central Powers.

By the end of 1915 construction of the 'Entrenched Camp' (or 'Birdcage' as its occupants called it) was almost complete. Its perimeter extended some 80 miles, much of it lakes and marshes presenting good obstacles. Despite Greek protests the Serbian army was shipped to Corfu to recover. The French General, Maurice Sarrail, was appointed Joint Allied commander at Salonika as further British reinforcements arrived from Gallipoli to join the 10th (Irish) Division in the 'Birdcage' and went to work on roads, docks, bridges and a railway. Sarrail's orders were to pin down German forces to prevent their transfer to Verdun on the Western Front. An advance out of the entrenched camp was planned for early March 1916 when the roads became passable. French and British accordingly pushed some 20 miles out of their positions towards the Bulgarian border. When Greek frontier troops handed over the key frontier fortress of Rupel to the Bulgarians in May without firing a shot in its defence the Allies realised that Greek neutrality was a negotiable commodity. Rising Greek dissent

over the presence of Franco-British troops on the frontier was exacerbated by the arrival from Corfu of 118,000 Serbian troops, re-equipped and eager to avenge recent defeats. At this point the Allies almost fell out. Sarrail had been ordered by his government to advance beyond the Greek frontier, in anticipation that Rumania was about to enter the war on the Allied side. The British local commander, General Milne, received

contradictory orders from London: to consider himself under Sarrail's orders only for operations in and around the 'Birdcage', and to refrain from crossing the Greek frontier. After much discussion Sarrail was told to advance, if necessary with French and Serbian forces only. His command had swollen with the arrival of a Russian contingent to a strength of 250,000, and in August a large Italian force joined the

Salonika army. Further to the west, in Albania, an Italian army corps faced the Austrians across the Voyusa river, where neither side took any action until the end of 1916.

In August 1916 Rumania had at last decided, fatally as it happened, to enter the war, and the Bulgars advanced to forestall the Allies offering help to their new colleague. Sarrail was under orders from Paris to check the Bulgars and to launch a

The collier *River Clyde* beached below Sedd-el-Bahr castle, one of the main Outer Forts at the entrance to the Dardanelles. On the morning of 25 April 1915 the Royal Munster Fusiliers and the Hampshire's attempted to land from her with the aim of storming the castle's defences. The exit ports in the ships sides can be clearly seen. However, these and the gangways down which the men had to leave the ship were covered by deadly rifle and machine gun fire and the landing was stopped after the Munsters has suffered appalling casualties. The Hampshire's went ashore early the next day and took the village and castle of Sedd-el-Bahr after ferocious fighting. (IWM)

counter-offensive in September. Only the French and Serbs took part, and the British remained in their positions on the Struma front. After fierce fighting in which the Serbs distinguished themselves the Bulgarian line was broken and in November the Serbs renewed their attack, forcing the Bulgars to evacuate the battered town of Monastir before the bitter winter forced an end to serious campaigning.

Rumania's decision to declare war on the Central Powers was calamitous. Falkenhayn, commanding the German 9th Army, dealt a series of shattering blows to the Rumanians, forcing them to retreat on Bucharest, and surrender early in the new year.

After the frictions of 1916 the Allies agreed on a defensive posture at Salonika. Sarrail's problems were increased by the Greeks, whose fully mobilised army was concentrated but static in Thessaly even though Bulgarian troops had crossed into Greek territory. King Constantine had fallen out with his Prime Minister Venizelos who was dismissed, fleeing on 25 September 1916 to Crete where he set up his own Provisional Government. Early in October he arrived by invitation in Salonika where his government was immediately recognised by the Allies. The king was now isolated, but still enjoyed considerable support in and around Athens.

The Allies began to act energetically against the Greek royalist government, seizing ships of the Royal Hellenic Navy despite riots in Athens inspired by the king's supporters. As three Venizelist battalions joined the Allied army, Germany issued a formal warning to Greece, alleging 'infringements of neutrality'. The gloom was briefly lifted by the capture of

Monastir, Sarrail claiming this to be '... the first French victory since the Marne', even though most of the fighting had been done by the Serbs, who showed their disgust by refusing to continue the advance when the campaign restarted in the spring of 1917.

The naval war in the Mediterranean

Problems of command, control and coordination afflicted the Allied naval staffs as much as their army colleagues. No Naval Staff, equating to the Army's General Staff, existed in the Royal Navy before 1912 and it would be 40 years before a truly Joint Central Staff was created in Whitehall. In 1914 the Admiralty was unaware that the Army's staff had been conducting highly secret staff talks with their French opposite numbers for many years in order to ensure the rapid deployment of an Expeditionary Force to the continent in the event of war.

The presence of two, then (from 1915) three major Allied navies in the Mediterranean raised many problems. Prominent among these were those of national pride and the absence of any command structure or common doctrine. Even the language of command was a matter for acute debate. It got worse when a Japanese naval squadron joined the British, French and Italian fleets.

The Mediterranean had long been regarded as a 'British Lake' thanks to the Royal Navy's prestigious fleet based on Malta. It now had to be carefully partitioned to give the participating fleets their areas of operational responsibility. Four each were allotted to Britain and France and the Italian navy was given three. The system was quite inflexible; if a valuable troopship under destroyer escort left one national zone it had to be picked up by a destroyer from another navy: U-boat commanders were not slow to acquire this intelligence and capitalised on it whenever a handover went amiss. Strong resistance by naval commanders to the institution of a convoy system led to appalling shipping losses as the U-boat campaign got under way.

Apart from the ex-German warships *Goeben* and *Breslau* the Ottoman navy possessed few modern ships other than some torpedo boats; the old Turkish battleship *Messudieh* was sunk off Chanak in December 1914 by the British submarine B-11 and

The former German battlecruiser *Goeben*, under Turkish colours, anchored in the Bosphorus, Constantinople, October 1914. With her escorting cruiser, *Breslau*, she had eluded the British Mediterranean fleet in August and made her way to Constantinople where they were (ostensibly) sold to the Ottoman government and embodied into the Turkish fleet. The German sailors, when ashore in Constantinople, wore the fez. Machine gun detachments from both ships served on the Gallipoli peninsula, notable during the fierce fighting at Helles. (IWM)

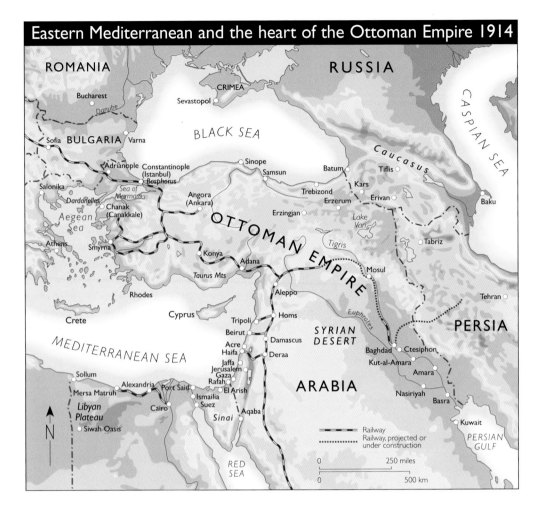

Eastern Mediterranean and the heart of the Ottoman Empire 1914

another pre-dreadnought, *Heiruddin Barbarossa* was torpedoed in the Sea of Marmara shortly after the Allied landings at Gallipoli. The saga of the *Goeben* remains an epic. Together with its escorting cruiser *Breslau* this modern battlecruiser had been very publicly on display at Constantinople in the summer of 1914 but slipped away for an unknown destination on the eve of the European war. It materialised off the French North African ports of Bone and Phillipeville to bombard them on 3 August 1914 before heading off to the east, impotently shadowed by the British Mediterranean fleet, which was unable to take action until Britain had formally declared war on Germany late on 4 August. Both ships evaded the pursuit and arrived off the Dardanelles to be given free passage up to Constantinople on the

orders of Enver Pasha, in flagrant breach of an international convention denying passage to foreign warships in time of war. Following the confiscation of the two Turkish super-dreadnoughts nearing completion in Britain, the Germans presented *Goeben* and *Breslau* to the Ottoman navy in a shrewd diplomatic move that did much to bring the Turks into the war on the side of the Central Powers. For much of the war they operated in the Black Sea, a considerable threat to the Russian fleet.

The Austro-Hungarian navy was based in the Adriatic, its capital ships securely bottled up there on Italy's entry into the war. These included several modern super-dreadnoughts of the Viribus Unitis class, each carrying 12 guns as main armament, more than a match for any of the pre-dreadnoughts of the Anglo-French fleet in the eastern Mediterranean. The Austrians were able to use a number of magnificent safe harbours and anchorages along their Adriatic coast, but the Italians had no safe naval bases on their east coast and it was easy for Austrian cruisers to carry out quick bombardment sorties against Italian coastal towns without fear of interception. The Italian navy possessed some modern dreadnoughts, based on Taranto and Brindisi in the south, but there were to be no major fleet actions. The Austrian battle fleet stayed at home and the Adriatic saw a war of small ships and submarines. In May 1915 the German *U-21* was the first to make the hazardous voyage from Germany to the Eastern Mediterranean; more followed, and soon flotillas of U-boats were based in Turkish and Austrian waters. Prefabricated parts of smaller submarines were sent from Germany overland for assembly at Cattaro, the main Austrian base, to play a significant part in the naval campaign.

By mid-May 1915, the arrival of German submarines in the Dardanelles area had tilted the balance dangerously. Following the loss of five elderly battleships – two to submarines, two to mines and one to a boldly handled torpedo boat, the remainder of the British fleet withdrew from close support of the troops ashore, reappearing off the beaches only for specific operations. An attempt was made to redress this deficiency later by sending out a number of monitors – shallow-draught ships carrying heavy-calibre guns, originally intended for operation in the shoal waters off the German coast and in the Baltic. Several of these were patrolling the entrance to the Dardanelles in 1918 when *Goeben* and *Breslau* made a final desperate sortie out into the Aegean; after blowing several of the monitors out of the water, both struck mines. *Breslau* sank with heavy loss of life and the damaged *Goeben* limped back to Constantinople where she remained for the rest of her long life as the flagship of a reconstituted Turkish navy, and in later years as an accommodation and training ship, finally going to the breakers in the 1960s.

The U-boats operating out of Cattaro worried the Allies to such an extent that they constructed a barrage across the Straits of Otranto. By mid-1916 it was in place. Over 100 fishing drifters and 30 motor launches patrolled the buoyed anti-submarine nets stretching across the gulf, dropping explosive charges when a submarine was detected. In the event only two submarines were destroyed in many hundreds of successful passages by the Cattaro U-boats. The drifters and motor boats were lightly armed with 57 mm guns; the captain of one gained the Victoria Cross when the Austrians made a rare sortie through the barrage, taking on a light cruiser at point blank range and miraculously surviving the loss of his boat, one of 14 lost on this occasion (before they sank them the Austrians chivalrously invited their crews to become prisoners of war). A scratch force of Allied destroyers vainly attempted to intercept the raiders and bring them to battle but skilful handling by their commander Captain Horthy (a future president of Hungary) enabled them to get home. Unlike the similar Dover Barrage whose destroyer guardships were permanently at sea, the Italian destroyers remained at anchor in harbour at Taranto. After the Austrian sortie the Italian admiral was sacked and the drifters were withdrawn from the barrage at night, enabling submarines to pass at will.

In the open Mediterranean, the Allied fleets struggled to ensure the free passage of merchant shipping essential to the war effort in the face of increasingly bold U-boat action. Under the terms of a convention signed by Britain, France and Italy, several combined fleets were created. There was still no agreed escort policy and casualties from U-boat action continued to rise. An ingenious ruse adopted by the Allies was to disguise harmless merchant ships as warships by adding wooden turrets, masts and funnels. One U-boat commander, believing he had torpedoed the British battle-cruiser *Tiger*, was astonished to see through his periscope that its guns, turrets and funnels were floating away as the ship went down.

The Austrian dreadnought *Szent Istvan* sinking after it had been torpedoed on 10 June 1918, 30 miles south of Pola. This was a particularly bold action on the part of a small Italian motor launch which got within 400 yards of its target before firing two torpedoes. Hit in the engine room, the battleship was left dead in the water and unable to use its pumps. As it heeled over, most of the crew managed to escape by walking over the keel as the ship turned turtle. (IWM)

In April 1917 the U-boat campaign in the Mediterranean reached a climax as 278,038 tons of Allied shipping went to the bottom with a further 113,000 tons severely damaged. It was decided to encourage merchant ships to sail by night, and to introduce a partial convoy system. Where appropriate, merchant shipping bound for the eastern Mediterranean from the United Kingdom was advised to use the Cape route, and intensified use of the Italian railway system was recommended. Twenty-eight U-boats were known to be based at Cattaro and Pola with the Kaiser's personal instructions to attack unescorted Allied hospital ships, a move foiled by attaching Spanish naval officers to their crews, thus granting neutral status.

The Allied fleets maintained a programme of shore bombardment against Austrian and Turkish installations, and the Italians developed the use of small motor torpedo boats to attack enemy ships in harbour. A notable success was achieved in December 1917 when two motor boats penetrated the defences at Trieste to sink the Austrian battleship *Wien*. In the following year this success was spectacularly repeated when motor boats torpedoed the super-dreadnought *Szent Istvan*, forcing the Austrians to cancel a planned sortie against the Otranto barrage. Further successful attacks were made against Austrian capital ships in the final weeks of the war, by which time the Emperor's navy was in a ferment of mutiny, but a gallant attempt to torpedo the former *Goeben* led to the loss of the British submarine *E-14* and the death of her captain, who was given a posthumous VC.

For the Allied navies the Mediterranean campaign had been one of steady application rather than dramatic fleet actions. But despite the difficulties of divided command and the lack of standardisation, the Austrian fleet that had been the chief threat was effectively prevented from exercising its power, and that of Turkey was neutralised from the start.

Cecil, Harold and Noel Wright

The Great World War of 1914–18 affected entire populations. Few families were spared the impact of the casualty lists publishing the dead, wounded and missing. One family in Christleton, a Cheshire village far from the battlefields, was typical.

Frederick Wright, a joiner, married Frances Tushingham in the 1880s, and they moved into a cottage in Quarry Lane. A large family duly arrived. Fred the eldest was followed by Marshall (Marsh), Harold, Hylton, Cecil, Noel, and finally three daughters: Effie, Amy and Eva. All the children attended the village school until their 14th year, when the boys sought work. The Wright boys found employment in Chester, three miles' walk away.

In 1907 a major overhaul of the Army and its reserve forces created the Territorial Force, which included the Earl of Chester's Yeomanry, originally raised in the 18th century for home defence. By the summer of 1914 Cecil was riding as a trumpeter with the regiment for its summer camp at Llangollen.Weeks later, on mobilisation, the yeomanry went to Northumberland to defend the coastline. They were still there a year later. Cecil wrote to his sister Eva from Morpeth Common camp in October 1915 describing the primitive conditions and appalling weather (spelling throughout the letters remains uncorrected):

It has rained for 28 hours without a stop, things are in a fine mess if it is only catching hold of the dirty wet headropes, it is rotten. I have finished transport driving and gone to the troop again. We do very little drill here, it is all road work, every other day we go between 40 and 50 miles we are seeing the countryside and a very nice country it is ... on Thursday we started at 6.30 am and landed back at 7.15 pm

just before dark, it was a lovely day and the Cheviot Hills looked fine ... PS the Scotchish Horse that was here before us went to the Front some at home may have been in the papers where they have been cut up.

(The Scottish Horse had been sent via Egypt to Gallipoli where they had to fight as infantry).

On one postcard dated 15 October 1915 Cecil added a message telling her that he had been promoted to corporal:

I believe we are going to the first line in a month or two. We have had a big week. The ground was covered with frost at 11 am so you can see what it is like sleeping in the open ...

Cecil's subsequent letters are all from Egypt and Palestine. Three of the Wright brothers served in that theatre. Noel transferred to the Royal Flying Corps as ground crew, and Harold served in the Royal Garrison Artillery (RGA). By May 1917 General Murray's Egyptian Expeditionary Force had slowly advanced up the Mediterranean coast into Palestine but had been repulsed in two attempts to take the town of Gaza. Harold wrote to his sister shortly after the second battle:

... don't think we are having a bad time here although there is a war on, for speaking the truth we are having a jolly good time at present ... I hope they forget us and leave us here for the duration. We get nothing else but sunshine from morning till night, we have blue glasses and short pants. The lanes are 3 inches deep in dust so when we were marching we got smothered and choked and we were not allowed to have a drink out of our water bottles and when we halted we dared not drink for it is a bad practice to drink water out here we just rinced our mouths out. We

Whit Monday 1917. The Wright brothers meet near Gaza (left to right) Harold, Noel, Cecil. They never met again. Cecil became an infantryman when the Cheshire Yeomanry (to their great grief) were unhorsed in Palestine to compensate for the loss of infantry battalions sent to the Western Front. He was also bound for France, on transfer to the King's Shropshire Light Infantry and died there of Spanish Influenza in November 1918, two days before the Armistice. (Author's collection)

rise in the morning and go on parade at 6 and have an hour on Swedish drill, then we have breakfast, oatmeal porridge, bacon and bread and good stuff it is and we wash it down with a pint of tea with plenty of sugar – the only thing we go short of is milk for cows are very scarce here. We go on parade again at 9 until 11.30 on the guns, a bit tiring owing to the heat. Then we go to the guns again from 3 to 4.30, getting cooler than, and we have finished the day'.

Shortly after this, by a happy coincidence, the three brothers managed to meet on Whit Sunday 1917 on the battlefield, an event celebrated with a photograph. It was the last time they would all be together.

Meanwhile, Cecil continued fighting and marching with the dismounted yeomanry. On the eve of the 3rd battle of Gaza he sent a card to Eva:

Well, I have not got much time as we are on the move tonight. All the movements are done at night, it's a lot better for marching in the cool. We are looking forward to the rainy season starting. You can take this for granted an infantryman out here never as a good time. We are starting tonight on this mobile stunt that means iron rations …

In a letter dated 22 November 1917 Harold described the recent battle of Gaza, although he also took the opportunity to complain that none of his sisters had written to him for weeks – 'how would you like it all my pals receiving letters from home and me having none you don't seem to realise what a letter means on a shell-riddled desert ...' He then goes on to describe the battle:

Now before the great advance I had a letter from Cecil to say he was ready, that meant to meet the Turkish army so you could tell what my feelings were when the great guns roaring and the Turkish shells flying not far from me, then to see the lights going up and lighting the earth for miles. Our artillery forming the barrage to clear the way for our infantry that were firing their rifles and charging with there bayonets. You at home don't seem to realise what a horrible clash it all is and me thinking how poor Cecil was going on. I knew he was in front but what part I did not know but I afterward found out that he was in the attack on Beersheba, that is where the Cheshire Yeo made there debut and they were received with a strong force of the Turkish army but they did not fail to do so for they put him on the run with there bayonets ... we have had some very hard strugles and our infantry must have had very hard times for we have had very hot weather considering it is well on in November and we have had some very wet days, marching in this country with a full pack is above all jokes but the scarcest thing of all is water but in spite of all these drawbacks we have chased him for miles, we are well past Jerusalem and Bethlehem ...

After the 3rd battle of Gaza the campaign slowed down. While Cecil was in a Cairo hospital with fever in April 1918, Harold met Noel in Alexandria where they lived in luxury for a couple of days:

Fancy me and Noel in Alex with bags of cash and Cecil stony in Cairo, me and Noel had a royal time, we did live, he only had two half days off but was out by 5.30 every night and we had supper together every day, it's a true saying that there's corn in Egypt but not only corn. To give you some idea, for breakfast, 4 eggs, bread, butter, and tea as much as I wanted for one shilling, for dinner which I had at the finest café in Alex, Chip potatoes, beef steak, two vegetables, and tea ... After tea we went for a stroll or the pictures, then for Supper we went to

a Posh café for coffee ... then I sent Noel home like some Lord going from his club in our open carriage and if that's not going the swank I don't know what is ...

However, despite this luxury, Harold was still homesick:

... but Eva, a leave here seeing all these sights is nothing, I would give you my word, I would rather have come to dear old Blighty and as cold as it is to stand in the food queues all day just to get amongst a little bit of civilisation and to here the Old English language spoken once more ...

Back in the desert conditions were harsh again:

Today there is a terrible sand storm so when we go out we have to wear sand goggles to protect our eyes or otherwise we would get nearly blinded and the flies are terrible while I am writing these lines they are in bunches on my hands and face I believe they are watching what I am writing about ...

When Allenby resumed the offensive Harold's battery was in constant action. His letters increasingly reflect his homesickness and the soldier's eternal complaint about mail from home. In July, from 'Somewhere in Judaea' he writes at length:

'You never wrote me a single line telling how you enjoyed yourself at "Whit" Monday. I was wondering Eva when I shall have that great pleasure of rowing on the Dee and listening to the band ... it's Saturday night 9 pm and I am on duty till Monday night on the telephone at the guns and we have just finished firing for Johnny [Turk] as given us a very rough time in our section today. He has done a deal of damage the shrapnel as been falling like rain and flashing like lightning but I am pleased to say they were falling ½ mile short of me. It's a fine sight watching them but not very pleasant stopping it according to what I could see Harry Culham and Frank Rowlands were having their full share I am anxiously waiting to hear all they have to say about it for we go visiting each

Trumpeter Cecil Wright, Cheshire Yeomanry, at the regiment's summer camp, North Wales, 1913. He would have been mounted on one of the hundreds of working horses 'impressed' under the terms of the Army Act from firms and farms all over Cheshire in order to equip the regiment for camp. In war, a comprehensive remounts service, run by retired army officers, went into action all over the United Kingdom and Ireland to select and purchase the thousands of additional animals needed to provide chargers, gun teams and draught horses. In peace, whenever the yeomanry went to annual camp, Chester was virtually brought to a halt, as all its cab horses had been taken over for two weeks. (Author's collection)

other when things are quiet. (PS Harry as been over tonight, Monday, he's alright).

Cecil had been posted from the Yeomanry to the Kings Shropshire Light Infantry on the Western front. After home leave he saw

much action until October 1918 when he fell sick with the virulent Spanish influenza sweeping Europe. Taken to a military hospital at Etaples near Le Havre he died on 9 November, two days before the Armistice. The telegram notifying his death was delivered to the family cottage at Christleton on the 11th, casting the Wrights into deep mourning as the rest of the village rejoiced.

In August Harold, his long epistles failing to draw a response, wrote to Eva calling her an 'ungrateful hussy' but as the Egyptian Expeditionary Force's campaign ended he wrote in mellower mood on 5 November:

Just a few lines to tell you I am still in Ismailia Egypt but returning to Palestine in a few days but I am pleased to say as you know I am not returning to fight. That is one great consolation for the scrapping finished last week so it only means going back to Ludd to rejoin my battery ... I don't think I will ever see any more fighting and a good thing too ...'

Two days later Harold wrote again:

Dear Eva, a few lines to let you know whilst I was commencing to write in the "Chester Hut" Ismailia, YMCA, it has been announced that Germany has signed an Armistice. With Loud Cheers and everybody sang (praise God from whom all blessings flow) ... and I am now longing for the day when I embark on the boat to sail for Good Old Blighty and be with you all at home and to remain ... get plenty of music ready for that happy day.

A week later, from Palestine, and unaware of Cecil's death, he described the celebrations of the previous week:

'How did you all receive the news. I hope you are not all suffering from shell shock. We got the great news at 5.30 pm on the 11th you see how quickly good news travels and it is approaching 4000 miles from home. It was received here as you can guess with loud cheers we nearly all went mad, they all sang songs, beat tins, and made bon-fires. The big guns fired blank cartridges and gun cotton but the anti-aircraft fired shrapnel so you can imagine what a time we had that night. But Eva that will be the night when we get safely home, we will have a jubilee, what do you say. The next time we meet will be in Good Old Chester. So keep smiling Eva, you will have a good time running to the station to meet us all in our turns. That will be great sport, what do you think ...

For the Wrights of Christleton at least, the war was over.

The crew of a 60-pounder gun of the Royal Garrison Artillery, Palestine, 3rd battle of Gaza. (Author's collection)

The loose ends of war

The years following the Armistice of 1918 brought to all the nations involved a host of new problems. The Allied blockade of the Central Powers had not been entirely effective, because Germany and the Austro-Hungarian Empire had both received much help (as had the Allies) from neutrals. Although geography had prevented a full blockade of the Ottoman Empire, its creaking infrastructure was unequal to the logistic loads placed upon it and this, combined with the closure of the Dardanelles and the elimination of the Turkish merchant fleet, contributed to its economic as well as military decline, and eventual defeat.

The causes of the Austro-Hungarian military defeat are not hard to find: the ethnic, religious and political diversities faced by the Habsburgs combined to overwhelm them by 1918. These problems distracted the government in Vienna whilst their armies were trying to cope with war on several fronts. The civilian population found its living conditions steadily eroding and starvation set in. Resistance to infection declined and when the influenza pandemic got under way in 1918 it decimated whole populations in central and eastern Europe. Food riots became commonplace in the cities of the empire and civil unrest spread to the armies, sapping their will to fight.

The outbreak of war in 1914 had been greeted enthusiastically on both sides; mobilisation of the huge continental armies took place in an euphoric atmosphere of bands, flowers stuck in rifle barrels, and patriotic songs. Poets saw the war in romantic terms. The better ones still spared a thought for the young men who would not return, but some produced doggerel of appalling quality, celebrating '... men going forth to die in martial ecstasy upon the bayonets'. In Germany the most popular theme was that of God's presence in support of fleets and armies; every German soldier bore the motto '*Gott mit Uns*' – God with us – on his belt buckle, and even Rupert Brooke felt moved to thank God for 'matching us to His Hour'. In the darkest hours of 1915 a note of elevated optimism is still evident in poems flooding back from the fronts. The Royal Naval Division at Gallipoli numbered several outstanding poets in its ranks, although Brooke had died of sickness in the Aegean on the eve of the April landings. Most had received rigorous classical educations and their works reflected a romantic attachment to the idea of fighting within sight of ancient Troy. Patrick Shaw-Stewart, himself to die on the Western Front in 1917, was a typical product of what must have seemed a coming golden age; educated at Eton and Balliol College Oxford, his friend Rupert Brooke thought him 'the most brilliant man they've had at Oxford for ten years'.

The early optimism and windy patriotism of the war poets evaporated for ever after the bloodbaths of Loos and Gallipoli in 1915 and the Somme in the following year. Sassoon, Graves, and above all Wilfred Owen, display a growing sense of futility, especially among the front-line soldiers and their officers. Even Rudyard Kipling, whose rousing words did much to stimulate recruiting in the first year of the war, changed his tone after his beloved only son, a subaltern in the Irish Guards, was lost at Loos. Thereafter, his works convey an elegiac sense of realisation that it is always the youth of a nation that pays the price for its politicians' ineptitude and pride.

Culture survived despite all else throughout Europe. Paradoxically the arts thrive in times of war, as people seek escape from grisly reality. England's leading composer Edward Elgar set numerous patriotic works to music; his occasional music for Imperial events like coronations and jubilees had already become widely known, and his adaptation of the 1st Pomp and Circumstance March to words by A C Benson gave the nation an alternative anthem: Land of Hope and Glory. For the first time, the Government appointed well-established artists to record all aspects of the war; the results of this imaginative enterprise, deposited at the Imperial War Museum in London, comprise one of the most comprehensive collections of 20th century British art to be found anywhere. The outstanding wartime work of Stanley Spencer, conceived when he was serving as a medical orderly in Macedonia, can be seen in mural form at a memorial chapel near Newbury.

Wars invariably lead to remarkable advances in technology, whether for destructive or benevolent purpose. In the latter case, medicine stands to benefit above all else, for it is a nation's interest to maintain the health of its people as well as to ensure that the maximum number of fighting men wounded in battle are returned to the firing line. The Great War of 1914–18 was probably the first in which deaths in battle exceeded those resulting from disease, but the Spanish influenza that devastated the world after 1918 probably killed more than all the battles put together. In the South African war of 1899–1902 over 60 per cent of the British dead had been from sickness, prompting the War Office to conduct searching examination of its medical services. Improved medical research in the first decade of the century resulted in greatly improved preventive measures in sanitation, control of infections, better education in personal hygiene, and inoculation against some of the most dangerous diseases including typhoid. In the first year of the war half Britain's doctors were mobilised, depriving many hospitals of their key personnel but ensuring that the armed forces received the best possible medical attention. Whether serving in uniform or in the teaching hospitals and research departments of universities, doctors were able to benefit from an explosion of innovation and discovery in medical science. Developments in radiology, anaesthesia, pathology, orthopaedics, plastic surgery and the psychiatric treatment of what became known as 'shell shock' led not only to vastly improved chances of survival for battle casualties, but in the longer term to improved standards of national health. Although the discovery of antibiotics lay years ahead, great advances were being made in the effective treatment of wounds using new antiseptic solutions that, unlike phenol or carbolic acid, would not damage human tissue.

If advances were being made by all the combatants in the treatment of battle wounds, the fight against disease went in parallel. At Salonika the Anglo-French forces were stricken by virulent strains of malaria; at Gallipoli, dysentery and typhoid claimed thousands of victims and in Mesopotamia the Indian troops were victims of deficiency disease brought about by inadequate diet. This brought about an urgent examination of the roles of the newly discovered vitamins. Before 1912 many doctors believed that beri-beri was caused by bacteria. Until it was found that vitamin B1, present in yeast, would arrest scurvy, the sepoys of the Indian Army in Mesopotamia were prostrated by this ailment. The deficiency in their rations made good by doses of Marmite, they rapidly recovered.

Inevitably, as the advances made in life-saving medical techniques were taken up by all the warring nations, so too was there rapid progress in military technology. Before 1914 Britain had relied on its navy as the sure shield of the nation; the army was regarded as an imperial gendarmerie, trained and equipped accordingly. Thus, when it was forced to take part in a gigantic war of attrition on the Western Front, it was out-gunned by a German army with superior artillery and vastly greater manpower. The advent of trench warfare presented the British and French general staffs with a seemingly intractable problem: how to break through the immensely strong German trench systems, protected as they were by wide belts of barbed wire covered by machine guns. The answer was the tank, developed in England and initially launched on the Somme in penny packets and over totally unsuitable terrain. Not until 1917 when several hundred broke through the German lines at Cambrai was it possible to see that a new era in land warfare had begun. Even so, the insistence of the high command that horsed cavalry should be used to exploit the success of the tanks – which they signally failed to do – reflects the conservatism of many generals at even this late stage of the war. Cavalry, the *Arme Blanche* whose role was shock action against infantry, had become obsolete overnight in the Franco-Prussian war of 1870–71 when they were mown down by a deadly combination of machine gun, quick-firing field artillery and the magazine rifle.

Battlefield tactics underwent a transformation after 1914. The British had attempted to apply mid-19th century battle drills against Boer marksmen on the South African veldt in 1899 and paid a dreadful price. In 1914 the Germans made the same mistake, pitting their massed columns against a British regular army that had learned its South African lesson and could bring controlled and highly accurate rifle fire to bear with devastating effect. Lethal in defence, the magazine rifle also enabled infantry to fight in extended order when in the attack, instead of in close order. Unhappily, this improvement was neutralised on 1 July 1916 when the British army left its trenches on the Somme and trudged towards the uncut German wire and machine guns.

Sea warfare had been changed forever by the launch of the world's first all-big-gun battleship, HMS *Dreadnought*, in 1906. Her arrival triggered off a race between Britain and Germany to equip their main battle fleets with ships of this power. In the event the long-expected clash, when it took place in the North Sea in June 1916, was inconclusive. What it did prove was that German technology had produced battleships well suited to such a slogging

match; their gunnery was superb and their ships better protected against plunging fire. The craft that actually influenced the war at sea more than any other was the formerly despised submarine. The Germans, effectively bottled up in its bases by the Allied blockade, sought to destroy their enemies' seaborne commerce and very nearly succeeded. While the great battle fleets of both sides spent the war in almost total idleness it was the destroyers and other anti-submarine ships that finally obtained the decision, and then only with the belated aid of the convoy system.

The innovations playing a part in the operations of all fleets were those for which Admiral Fisher had fought so relentlessly against deeply entrenched conservatism in the Royal Navy and Admiralty: oil fuel, steam turbine propulsion, submarines, tethered mines, torpedoes, naval aviation, wireless telegraphy and radical new methods of officer selection and training. Few serving officers in any navy in 1918 would have dared to prophesy that of all these, it would be naval aviation and the aircraft carrier that would win decisive naval campaigns of the next war in the distant Pacific.

The Wright brothers had made their first unsteady flight at Kittyhawk a bare 11 years before the Archduke Franz Ferdinand met his untimely end at Sarajevo. All major armies in Europe had set up air wings before 1914 but the initiative rested with the Germans until 1916, when the Allies at last developed the essential device enabling machine guns to be mounted to fire forward through the propeller. In the opening months of the war, aircraft were limited to the reconnaissance and spotting roles but air-to-air combat soon ensued, demanding ever-heavier armament and higher performance from the combat aircraft. The British Expeditionary Force went to France in August 1914 with less than 100 machines. By April 1918 when the RFC and Royal Naval Air Service were merged to form the Royal Air Force, thousands of aircraft and no less than 30,000 spare engines had been constructed. Heavy bombers were being used by both sides to bomb their opponents' homelands; the dawn of the strategic bomber offensive. Proponents of air power – Trenchard in Britain, Emilio Douhet in Italy, and Brigadier General Billy Mitchell in the United States – confidently forecast that in any future war navies and armies would be subordinate to the air arm and that 'the bomber would always get through'.

As boulders hurled into still waters generate ever-widening ripples, the fighting on the Western and Eastern Fronts between 1914 and 1918 can be seen as the biggest stones; but the campaigns around the shores of the Mediterranean and its hinterlands may be seen as lesser pebbles whose ripples interacted on each other, in ways that significantly affected the outcome of the main contest, bringing down the German and Austro-Hungarian empires, and with them, that of the Ottomans. The peace secured at Versailles was illusory, as it failed to extinguish the embers of nationalism that would plunge western Europe into a yet more bloody war. America's failure to join the League of Nations helped to ensure the rise of Fascism, for none of the member states was prepared to act against Mussolini and Hitler as they launched their respective aggressions in the 1930s. The rise of Arab nationalism would lead to seemingly insoluble problems in the Middle East. Even decisive wars create as many new problems as they solve old ones.

War on the home front

The Great War was a watershed in British society, affecting every family and home in the United Kingdom, as in all the combatant nations. In the village of Christleton most able-bodied men were serving by the end of 1915 in far-flung theatres of war. Three of the Wright brothers were in the Near East. On the strength of the meagre training in his school cadet corps Brian Hickey, the parson's son, was

given a commission in the county regiment and was posted to the 11th Cheshires in France in midsummer 1916. Families at home had to come to terms not only with the absence of breadwinners but also the need to generate income. Men found medically unfit for the armed forces were directed into work supporting the war effort. Frederick Wright senior and his eldest son, as skilled workers, worked on the construction of the huge hutted camps springing up in every district; in their case around Wrexham just across the county border. Their womenfolk had to get on with running the family home despite growing shortages of foodstuffs. These shortages were caused by the German U-boats,

Fred, Amy and Eva Wright and Corporal Cecil Wright – taken during his last leave home, 1918. Eva was then 17, Fred, who had had a mastoid operation, was medically unfit for military service. In any case, his skills as a woodworker placed him in a 'reserved occupation' and thus immune from conscription after this had been introduced in 1916. (Author's collection)

which in April 1917 sank 25 per cent of all ships leaving British ports, a total of a million tons. Domestic food supplies were affected and in that summer huge queues formed outside Chester's butchers and grocers. In the early spring the national reserve of grain had been down to six weeks. The vital supply of pit props from neutral Scandinavia was also affected, causing the government to set up the Forestry Commission with a remit to grow the timber needed for the mines. Faced with continuing shipping losses the Admiralty was forced to adopt the convoy system, which immediately stabilised the crisis in the Atlantic – but not in the Mediterranean where it was not fully implemented.

It was clear by the end of 1917 that food distribution in the UK was haphazard, producing great inequalities, especially in the industrial towns of the Midlands and north. Bread had already risen to a price of 10 pence a loaf, depriving the very poor of a basic foodstuff. The Government ordered higher wheat extraction rates to give more flour but the resultant 'national' loaf, being off-white, proved unpopular. Trades unionists staged demonstrations in Hyde Park against rising food prices and early in 1918 a rationing scheme was introduced under the auspices of Lord Rhondda at the new Ministry of Food. Each citizen was issued with a book of coupons, to be handed over the counter when paying for a given quantity of sugar, meat or butter. Additional foodstuffs were placed on the ration as necessary. Margarine, on ration, went on general sale as an unpalatable butter substitute. The scheme was accepted by the people as an equitable way of ensuring that all got their fair share, even though little or no attempt was made by the authorities to audit the huge piles of coupons handed over to local food offices by grocers and butchers. Legislation enabling the government to introduce and enforce such measures stemmed from the notorious Defence of the Realm Act, known as DORA, hurriedly enacted by Parliament in August 1914 and thereafter employed as the catch-all giving powers of requisition of property, the

enforcement of conscription for military and industrial service, and the arrest and detention of anyone suspected of unpatriotic activities. It was held by many to be a denial of basic civil liberties. As the war went on it was used to impose food controls and public house licensing hours (to counter the wave of drunkenness among workers in the war industries). The rector of Christleton, as secretary of the Chester Diocesan Temperance Association, considered it his patriotic duty to enrol the youth of the parish into its ranks, issuing Eva Wright and her sisters with certificates pledging themselves to lives of total abstinence.

The impact of war on a village like Christleton came gradually. Fields had to be tilled and as the war continued, county agricultural committees, usually chaired by the big landowners and squirearchy, endeavoured to increase yields; they and the government were all too aware that a national farmers' strike would bring the nation to its knees, once the U-boat campaign had begun to bite. By 1916, women were working on the land, tackling jobs hitherto performed only by men. As in the factories, where the productivity of women workers consistently exceeded that of men, they were initially treated with ridicule, soon changing to grudging admiration.

The early battles involved only the regular army, but with the arrival of the Territorials and Yeomanry at the front, familiar names began to appear on casualty lists and almost every Sunday the rector announced from the pulpit that another local man had been killed or gone missing. In October 1916 his own son's name joined the lists. Second Lieutenant Hickey had been severely wounded on the eve of his 19th birthday when a shell burst in the trench where he and his men were preparing for a major assault. Although church leaders repeatedly urged the nation to turn to God, the blurring of class distinctions that took place during the war years had begun to erode the influence of the churches. The relaxation of time-honoured social taboos led to huge increases in illegitimacy and in the incidence of prostitution and venereal disease, especially in garrison towns, and in the areas where huge hutted training camps had been set up. When peace came, the whole social structure had changed beyond recall. There had been a time when village girls had little choice but to enter domestic service on low pay and with little chance of bettering themselves. As the school-leaving age was raised to 14, a better-educated generation of young women raised their expectations too. Eva Wright and her sisters could not wait to apply for jobs as shop assistants in Chester as soon as they were 18. Although the militant and often violent campaign of the pre-war Suffragette movement led by Mrs Pankhurst had alienated much of the population, she and her supporters had given their wholehearted support to the war effort, in particular the use of women in industry, agriculture, transport and in the new uniformed auxiliary services. The enthusiastic response of the nation's women to the war, described by Mrs Pankhurst as 'God's vengeance on the people (ie men) who held women in subjection' was to gain the vote in 1918 for those over 30 and eventually for all over 21.

Enemy air action against England during the first three years of the war was almost entirely limited to raids by Zeppelin airships. These caused some damage in London and in the east coast towns, but on occasion one or two reached the Manchester and Liverpool areas, leading to the imposition of domestic and industrial black-out measures. Mrs Wright and her daughters sewed their own thick curtains, purchased in the sales at Brown's, Chester's main department store. Prudently set aside in 1918 they were to see service again in 1939. Writing from the Somme two weeks before he was wounded, the rector's son, not without a touch of irony, expressed his pleasure that '... the Zeppelins didn't bomb the house or the tennis courts', adding that 'I am as lousy as it is almost possible to get and would be very pleased if you could send me a tin of Boots's "Vermin in the Trenches", which I am told is a good thing to have about one ...'

Noel (seated) and Harold Wright on leave in Alexandria in April 1918. Noel is wearing the distinctive tunic of the Royal Flying Corps and Harold the uniform of the Royal Garrison Artillery: breeches, puttees, spurs and crossbelt with ammunition pouches. Harold describes their brief leave together in letters to his sister, Eva of Christleton, Chester. Cecil, the third of the brothers serving in the Middle East at that time was unable to join the others as he was sick in a Cairo hospital. Shortly after this he was sent to the Western Front in France. (Author's collection)

After almost four years, and despite the efforts of the government to keep up the nation's spirits, war weariness set in. Civilians were urged in 1918 to observe one meatless day a week (the army capitalised on this with recruiting posters offering recruits 'Meat every Day!'). The civilian ration had been reduced by then to one pound of sugar, one and a half pounds of meat and a few ounces of fat, margarine or butter a week. This was sufficient to maintain reasonable health levels, unlike in the blockaded states of the Central Powers where many starved, and disease due to poor nutrition prepared the way for the influenza pandemic that was about to sweep Europe. The influenza killed Cecil Wright, whose family received the dreaded telegram announcing his death in France as Christleton church bells rang out for victory on the 11th day of November.

All through the war years the Wrights had sustained their spirits by home-made entertainment round the parlour piano; one of the songs they sang was the great hit 'Keep the Home Fires Burning', written by one Ivor Novello, an officer in the Royal Naval Air Service who, as Ivor Davies, had been a chorister with Brian Hickey at Magdalen College Oxford in the reign of King Edward VII. The cinema had begun to capture audiences that had formerly packed the galleries – the 'Gods' – of the music halls, whose days were numbered. Chester enjoyed a thriving cultural life throughout the war, based on its choral societies, its amateur orchestra and operatic society. Visiting theatre and opera companies – notably the Carl Rosa – performed the stock repertoire and the Wright sisters long remembered Mascagni's 'Cavaliera

Rusticana' in a particularly dire rendition that reduced the audience in the 'Gods' to helpless laughter. The people of Christleton thought nothing of walking the three miles into town and back for these treats.

With peace came the homecoming of the men who had survived four years of fighting in places they would never see again; indeed, most of the men from Christleton who served in the ranks had never been beyond the county boundaries before 1914. Their service had broadened their perspectives but all were adamant that they would never undergo the experience again. The Wright brothers settled down into their civilian jobs. Employment was still high, and in any case they were skilled men, capable of holding down jobs in a booming building trade. In December 1918 women over 30 voted for the first time in a general election called immediately after the Armistice by the wily Lloyd George, who asked the electorate to vote for his list of Liberal and Conservative candidates bearing what former Prime Minister Asquith (who lost his seat) caustically called the 'coupon of approval'. Lloyd George swept back into power with 479 MPs against an opposition of 229 and promptly reneged on virtually all his election promises; the 'Land fit for Heroes' did not materialise and the stage was set for years of industrial and economic unrest as a Britain in decline became a debtor nation. The landowners and industrial magnates who had lived in the larger houses in and around Christleton had lost their sons, and Brian Hickey his closest friends, on the battlefields of France and Flanders, Gallipoli and Palestine. The domestic staff who had serviced these families were no longer available, and in a harsher economic climate the formerly wealthy families decayed and departed.

End of the tragedy

The death of the aged Austrian Emperor on 21 November 1916 was the end of an era. His long reign had been punctuated by personal tragedy and the Vienna of his youth, enriched by a gaiety and culture unmatched elsewhere in Europe, was no more. Austrian national morale was sinking and the Allied blockade had brought the empire to the brink of starvation. The new Emperor Charles inherited an unhappy situation.

Fighting broke out in Athens at the beginning of December 1916 between troops still loyal to the king, and Allied sailors and marines. Allied ambassadors called on the king and delivered a 24-hour ultimatum to the royalist government. Reluctantly, the Greek army began to pull out of Thessaly under Anglo-French supervision. In reply, a royal warrant was issued for the arrest of Venizelos who for good measure was anathematised by the Patriarch Archbishop of Athens. A vicious campaign of assassination was directed against the prime minister's supporters. 'Between me and the King', commented Venizelos, 'there is now a lake of blood'. More Allied troops arrived at Salonika, where Sarrail planned to renew the offensive as soon as the roads were passable. The results were not encouraging. Two British divisions failed to break into the German-Bulgar positions at the end of April but Sarrail went ahead with his offensive on 5 May. A British night attack on the Doiran front failed due to the Bulgars' skilful use of searchlights, and the Serbs' refusal to advance after suffering over 14,000 casualties for little gain brought the offensive to a halt.

The struggle for power in Greece came to a head. King Constantine abdicated following the Allied ultimatum and was succeeded by his second son Alexander. Venizelos returned as prime minister, his first act being to declare war on the Central Powers.

The summer heat of 1917 brought thousands of casualties from disease at Salonika. The Struma valley was notorious for a particularly lethal strain of malaria and the British had to pull back to higher ground in an attempt to reduce the numbers of the sick, which by October had reached 21,000. Disease and lack of leave triggered mutinies in the French contingent. After months of complaints from the other Allies, Sarrail was finally replaced in December by General Marie Louis Guillaumat, who succeeded within weeks in repairing all the damage wrought by the slippery Sarrail by visiting all units under his command and re-invigorating the jaded Allied force. His opportunity to show his skills as a field commander was denied when, in June 1918, he was summarily recalled to Paris by his government without reference to the other Allies, and replaced by General Louis Franchet d'Esperey. The great German offensive on the Western Front drained the Salonika force of troops. As more Greek troops went into the line at Salonika it was possible to send 20,000 French and British troops to France.

Sporadic fighting had been in progress throughout 1917 in Albania where Italian troops, sent there without reference to the other Allies, had established a coastal bridgehead. In the summer of 1918, supported by the Royal Air Force, they attacked the Austrians north of Valona. A counter-attack in August drove them back, the last military success enjoyed by the Austro-Hungarian Empire.

In Macedonia the final Allied offensive got under way in September across the River Vardar. The Bulgarian Chief of Staff, General Lukov, suggested to Tsar Boris that he sue for peace, to be told to '... go out and die in your present positions'. By 17 September the

Bulgarian army that had fought hard and well for three years began to disintegrate as whole units mutinied and made for home. The Anglo-French attack on the Doiran, however, met furious resistance, the British suffering heavily. In the 65th Brigade of the 22nd Division only 200 men survived. The attack was renewed on the following day, failing again when 'friendly fire' halted the British advance. General Milne informed General d'Esperey that his men could do no more; in any case no more was required, as the Bulgars were broken. RAF aircraft reported on 21 September that huge columns were heading home in disarray, and a week later the Bulgarian government sought armistice terms, signing them on the 29th.

There was one last act. On 7 October the Allied Supreme War Council directed Milne to lead the Salonika Army eastward through Thrace and on to Constantinople. The Turks had already decided to seek an armistice, and this was duly signed on 30 October as the other Central Powers crumbled into defeat.

Aftermaths

It was soon apparent that the defeat of the Central Powers and their ally Turkey had failed to achieve the sort of lasting peace envisaged by idealists like President Wilson, whose enthusiasm for the League of nations was at once undermined by America's refusal to join.

The results of the war as they affected the former Mediterranean theatre succeeded, if anything, in producing a worse state of anarchy than had existed in 1914. Austria had good cause to regret her headlong rush into war against Serbia, for she suffered proportionately far greater loss than any other nation. Of 7.8 million men mobilised in the Habsburg Empire no less than 90 per cent were killed, died of sickness, were wounded, taken prisoner or missing in battle (by comparison, Britain's losses came to just under 39 per cent of those in uniform). Political disintegration was already evident in Vienna months before the Armistice. Reluctant recognition of a Czech Republic had been granted in April 1918 and the promise of independence for other Habsburg minority nations by the Allies had further undermined the Austrian position. The proclamation of the Austrian Republic on 13 November 1918 spelt the end for the Habsburgs and was immediately followed by the proclamations of the Hungarian Republic and the United Kingdom of Serbs, Croats and Slovenes. With the drastic curtailment of her borders Austria became a landlocked German state. Cut off from its previous sources of raw materials and hedged by vengeful tariff barriers imposed by the victors, the young republic was no longer a sound economic entity and unrest soon spread. Unification with Germany, the obvious solution, was prohibited by the Allies; social and political instability prevailed and a failed Nazi coup in 1934 served only to hasten the inevitable German invasion of 1938, which was overwhelmingly endorsed by a plebiscite.

In the Balkans, old scores remained to be settled. The Serbs soon revived their efforts to bring Yugoslavia under their control, despite the ferocious resistance of Croats and Slovenes. Desperately trying to bring a measure of stability, King Alexander imposed a dictatorship in 1929; it brought temporary relief but still left the Serbs in a powerful position and he was assassinated at Marseilles in 1934 by a member of one of the dissident minorities. Even worse chaos prevailed in Albania through the 1920s until President Ahmed Bey Zogu proclaimed himself king as Zog I. Trying to modernise his primitive realm, he was making reasonable progress until April 1939 when an Italian invasion forced him into exile.

The political infighting in Greece between King George II and premier Venizelos continued for years. Following its defeat in its ill-starred war with Turkey Greece agreed to a massive exchange of populations; over 1.25 million Greeks left Asia Minor as Turks returned from the former Ottoman provinces in Greece. The hapless Armenians of eastern Anatolia paid a dreadful price for their support of Russia and the western Allies during the Great War and at least a million died in uncontrolled massacres. Greece lurched unsteadily from kingship to republicanism, an uneasy truce prevailing between Venizelos the dedicated nationalist and his king. The prime minister was not finally ousted until 1928 after an unexpected electoral rout, and he died in exile in 1936, following the return of George II to the throne.

Italy had suffered losses in battle of 600,000 dead and had high hopes of reward from the Allies. These were soon dashed; apart from a grudging grant of some Austrian territory there were to be no gifts of ex-German colonies. Britain and France did not feel generous toward Italy. They regarded Italy's conduct in sending troops over to Albania at the height of the war, and an expeditionary force to southern Turkey in 1919 before any treaties had been ratified as irresponsible. Political chaos took over in Italy as socialists, smarting under national humiliation and faced by the forces of conservatism and the Church, split into new factions. The new man was Benito Mussolini, who took advantage of the situation to launch his Fascist party, which took power in Milan in 1922, then marched on Rome where King Victor Emmanuel invited Mussolini to form a government.

By the time General Harrington and the British occupation force left Constantinople in 1923 Mustafa Kemal was strengthening his grip on the Turkish political scene. He had a vision for his country's future and pushed it through with remarkable energy. Since the defeat of the Greeks and their expulsion from Anatolia and Turkish Thrace he and his *coterie* of hand-picked supporters had worked untiringly to create a new constitution and to liberalise the entire country, now freed of the encumbrances of its former Arab and Balkan dependencies. By the time of his death in 1938 he had largely succeeded; the Arabic alphabet had been abolished, together with many other relics of Ottoman days like the fez. Education programmes were abolishing illiteracy, women enjoyed their new-found rights, and with the abolition of the Caliphate Turkey became a secular state, its constitution firmly upheld by the army: the 'school of the nation' in which all young men were required to serve as conscripts. In all these drastic reforms Kemal, now known as Ataturk – father of the Turks – was backed by well-tried colleagues like General Ismet, victor of the battle of Inonu over the Greeks. When Kemal ruled that all Turks should take a surname Ismet adopted the name of his great victory and, as President Inonu, succeeded Ataturk in 1938.

In 1918 it had seemed that the Hashemite dynasty, staunch allies of Lawrence in the Desert war of the Hedjaz, would reap their just reward and become rulers of much of Arabia and Transjordan. History decreed otherwise. Emerging from Kuwait in 1925 the al-Saud family and their followers seized the holy places of Islam, the cities of Mecca and Medina, and also the port of Jeddah, establishing a firm grip over the Muslim pilgrimage trade, and enforcing adherence to the principles (if not always the strict practice) of puritanical Wahhabi Islam. The careful and often cynical planning of French and British agents in the war years had turned to dust and the future shape of Arabia rested with the Saudis.

Britain's influence in Egypt dated back to 1882 and was tolerated by the majority of the population for 30 years; although nominally still part of the Ottoman Empire in 1914 the country prospered as a British protectorate and had been formally declared such in December 1914. Since 1882 great steps had been made in irrigation, provision of an infrastructure of roads and railways, and education. The British had scrupulously respected the Muslim faith and the educated classes were mostly compliant. But during the war years, when the British had resorted to mass conscription for ill-paid labour and had requisitioned vast quantities of useful material, a nationalist movement had burgeoned. Its political party was the *Wafd* and its programme was independence. Deportations of its leaders led to serious insurrection, put down vigorously by the British army under Field Marshal Allenby who was appointed High Commissioner in 1919. As the result of a Commission headed by Lord Milner, independence was proposed, subject to guarantees for British interests, principally those concerned with the Suez Canal. Britain terminated the protectorate in 1922 but kept a military presence. Discussions between the two countries continued intermittently, resulting in a treaty of 1936 in which Britain reserved the right to maintain a garrison in the Canal Zone.

In Britain the postwar years were troubled. The nation was tired and bankrupt. The men returned to anything but the 'Land fit for

Heroes' promised by that most glib of politicians Lloyd George. The Wrights of Christleton mourned for Cecil as his brothers took up their trades, mostly in the building industry, to live out their uneventful lives in peace. Cecil's grave at Etaples was visited by members of the family in 1985 and a cutting taken from a rosemary bush growing by his headstone was brought home; it flourishes still as a living war memorial in a Hampshire country garden. The three Wright sisters all lived to great ages; Effie, the last survivor of that large family, stayed on in the village until her nineties.

Brian Hickey the parson's son was so badly wounded, and then almost burnt to death in a hospital fire, that he saw no more active service. In 1920 he became a teacher at Heatherdown, an exclusive preparatory school at Ascot. He continued to go back to Christleton on his Sunbeam motor cycle, not only to visit his parents at the rectory but also to pay court to Eva Wright. They were married, in the teeth of opposition from both families, in 1927.

The various campaigns around the Mediterranean failed in the end to divert much attention from the Western Front where the final decisions were fought out, and where the British army under Haig would win the greatest victory in its long history. The collapse of the Ottoman, Austro-Hungarian and German empires was followed all too soon by that of the British. The Near East faced decades of strife with the rise of Zionism and the conflict with the claims of the palestinian Arabs. mussolini's Italy over-reached its expansionist aims by invading Abyssinia, and teh political strength that could only have arisen from American participation, stood helpless as the world slithered back to destruction in the 1930s.

Further reading

Note: This list contains only the bare references; all the books listed contain their own bibliographies; almost all the senior commanders produced their own memoirs and autobiographies which, in the nature of things, are of variable quality. British regimental histories frequently tend to be works of pious hagiography but are nonetheless of great interest, especially to the descendants of those named therein.

General overview

Churchill, W.S., *The World Crisis*. 4 volumes, (London, 1923–27). Splendidly written in its author's inimitable style, and with the insight of one who was seldom far from the centre of things throughout the conflict. It is, however, far from objective in its assessment of the Gallipoli and Dardanelles campaign for the shortcomings of which many historians hold him to blame.

Crutwell, C.M.R.F., *A History of the Great War*. A sober and scrupulous account by an Oxford history professor. Elegant in style and balanced in judgement, it has been derided by a number of 'progressive' modern historians with little or no experience of actual war, but is regaining its standing with serious scholars.

Keegan, John, *The First World War*. (London 1998). A dazzling, if at times strongly opinionated, account.

Pitt, B., and Young, P., ed., *Purnell's History of the First World War*. Issued serially, (London, 1969–71). Superbly illustrated, with contributions from many distinguished historians, and particularly good on the so-called 'sideshows' such as the Balkan and Turkish campaigns.

Palestine, Egypt and Arabia

Falls, C., *Armageddon 1918*. (London 1964). The author was one of the official historians appointed by the Cabinet after 1918 and later became Chichele Professor of War at Oxford. His account is predictably analytic and academic but nevertheless most readable.

Lawrence, T.E, *Revolt in the Desert*. (Various publications). Highly dramatic personal account of the guerrilla campaign waged by Lawrence of Arabia and his Hashemite allies against the Turks, it is one of the great classics of military history and far more objective that the same author's autobiographical account in *Seven Pillars of Wisdom*.

Official History: Falls, C., *Military Operations, Egypt and Palestine*, 2 volumes, (London, HMSO, 1930).

Wavell, A,P., *The Palestine Campaign*. (London 1928). Lord Wavell's reputation as a historian was made by this and his short biography of General Allenby. A standard text book in many staff colleges, it remains the outstanding concise analysis of the campaign that broke the Ottoman army.

Italy

Falls, C., *Caporetto*. (London 1966).

Official History: Edmonds, J.E., & Davies, H.R., *Military Operations, Italy 1915–1919*, (London, HMSO, 1949).

Gallipoli and the Dardanelles

R Rhodes James: *Gallipoli*. (London 1965). Particularly lucid on the political and strategic aspects of the doomed attempt to take Constantinople and even-handed in its judgements of the politicians involved, particularly Winston Churchill.

Hickey, M., *Gallipoli*. (London 1995). A general survey of the campaign drawing on many hitherto unused sources, and numerous walking tours of the Gallipoli battlefields.

Liman von Sanders: *Five Years in Turkey*. (London 1928). Memoir of the outstanding German commander who master-minded the revival of the Turkish army from 1913 and later commanded the Ottoman armies in Palestine.

Official History: Aspinall-Oglander, ed., *Military Operations, Gallipoli*. 2 Volumes, HMSO (London, 1929–1932).

Mesopotamia

Official History: Moberly, F.J., *The Campaigns in Mesopotamia*, 4 volumes, Committee of Imperial Defence, (London, 1923–27).

Macedonia

Official History: Falls, C., *Military Operations, Macedonia*. Committee of Imperial Defence. 4 volumes. (London 1935).

Palmer, A., *The Gardeners of Salonika*. (London, 1966). A minor classic, describing life in the so-called 'entrenched perimeter' otherwise known by its inmates as the Birdcage.

Index

Related titles & companion series from Osprey

ESSENTIAL HISTORIES (ESS)
**Concise overviews of major wars
and theatres of war**

ELITE (ELI)
**Uniforms, equipment, tactics and personalities
of troops and commanders**

CAMPAIGN (CAM)
**Strategies, tactics and battle experiences
of opposing armies**

ORDER OF BATTLE (OOB)
**Unit-by-unit troop movements and
command strategies of major battles**
Contact us for more details – see below

NEW VANGUARD (NVG)
**Design, development and operation
of the machinery of war**

MEN-AT-ARMS (MAA)
**Uniforms, equipment, history
and organisation of troops**

AIRCRAFT OF THE ACES (ACES)
**Experiences and achievements
of 'ace' fighter pilots**

AVIATION ELITE (AEU)
Combat histories of fighter or bomber units
Contact us for more details – see below

WARRIOR (WAR)
**Motivation, training, combat experiences
and equipment of individual soldiers**

COMBAT AIRCRAFT (COM)
**History, technology and crews
of military aircraft**
Contact us for more details – see below

To order any of these titles, or for more information on Osprey Publishing, contact:
Osprey Direct (UK) *Tel:* +44 (0)1933 443863 *Fax:* +44 (0)1933 443849 *E-mail:* info@ospreydirect.co.uk
Osprey Direct (USA) c/o MBI Publishing *Toll-free:* 1 800 826 6600 *Phone:* 1 715 294 3345
Fax: 1 715 294 4448 *E-mail:* info@ospreydirectusa.com
www.ospreypublishing.com